For Lynn and Randal —

Enjoy!

Liesl.

Essence

of Home

Timeless Elements of Design

Liesl Geiger

Texts by
Richard Gluckman
and Ted Flato

THE MONACELLI PRESS

For Chris

First published in the United States of America in 2007 by
The Monacelli Press, Inc.
611 Broadway, New York, New York 10012

Library of Congress Cataloging-in-Publication Data
Geiger, Liesl.
Essence of home : timeless elements of design / Liesl Geiger ;
foreword by Richard Gluckman ; afterword by Ted Flato.
p. cm.
ISBN 978-1-58093-196-0 (hardcover)
1. Architect-designed houses—United States.
2. Architectural design—United States. 3. Architects
and patrons—United States. I. Title.
NA7205.G45 2007
728.0973—dc22
2007019127

Printed and bound in China

Produced by Chris Kincade

Designed by Pure+Applied
www.pureandapplied.com

FOREWORD 7 Richard Gluckman

INTRODUCTION 9

Design Origins 11

26 BARTLIT RESIDENCE
Lake/Flato Architects

Site and Scale 35

52 CANYON HOUSE
Steven Ehrlich Architects

60 CHILMARK HOUSE
Charles Rose Architects

Language and Style 69

90 DIAMOND A RANCH
Peter Pennoyer Architects

Openings and Light 99

118 HOUSE IN CABO SAN LUCAS
Steven Harris Architects

126 HOUSE IN MAINE
Toshiko Mori Architect

Spheres of Living 133

150 LEXTON MacCARTHY RESIDENCE
Lorcan O'Herlihy Architects

Flow of Space 159

174 MATCHBOX HOUSE
Gluckman Mayner Architects

182 SEMAPHORE HOUSE
Turner Brooks Architect

Sustainability 191

208 VILLA ON THE NEW JERSEY SEASHORE
Ike Kligerman Barkley Architects

AFTERWORD 217 Ted Flato

RESOURCES 218

Foreword

If part of architecture is the subjective application of objective criteria, then the part of architecture that deals with the design of a home becomes even more "subjective" with the participation of the client.

When an architect is faced with the task of designing an institutional project such as a library, school, or museum, the list of objective criteria can be complex and explicit. The design process of a large project has precise benchmarks at which programmatic, judicial, and a multitude of technical issues need to be resolved. These, together with the pressure of the budget and schedule, affect the fragile premise of a cohesive architectural design.

One of the architect's primary activities is to build a broad consensus across the wide range of constituents involved in a large-scale project. A residential project has many of the same criteria but is usually approached in a much simpler way. The consensus building is with a much more focused and active participant: the client.

The subjective criteria of the client directly influence the architect's direction. That is, the idea of home has a different meaning for different people. The idea of home can have many determinates: a childhood memory, a dynamic image in an architectural journal, an impression from a specific experience.

Liesl Geiger has assembled a strong group of architects. Each applies a distinct strategy in the projects shown here. None may be categorized as having a signature "style"; however, all share certain attributes, including a commitment to their profession, a research-based attitude within their practice, and a willingness to include the client as a participant in the very subjective process of designing a home.

The best clients are those who can realistically state their objective criteria and give shape to their subjective criteria, those who push the architect to explore alternatives and who step back at the critical point in the design process to allow the architect the final decision. This book will go a long way toward making better clients and toward making the collaborative exercise a successful adventure.

Richard Gluckman
Gluckman Mayner Architects

The dining room of the Matchbox House on Long Island, designed by Gluckman Mayner Architects, opens to an elevated porch.

Introduction

When I began this book, the importance of the relationship between architect and client was on my mind. I had just started building my own practice and was turning years of work with other architects into a personal vision. Previously, I had helped design projects ranging from Mediterranean-influenced farmhouses in Napa to contemporary Manhattan spaces inspired by light, space, and texture. Each new home had given me tools for creating meaning and language, and I wanted to find ways to distill the process of design into a framework.

Today's home is a richly varied synthesis, playing upon and incorporating modern, traditional, classical, regional, sustainable, stylish, inventive, and comfortable elements. It reflects the more informal lifestyles, environmental concerns, and diverse stylistic and practical influences that are changing the way we think about personal space. Houses today are both innovative and grounded. They engage the senses with strong connections to the land, its contours, its winds. They are imaginative and light in spirit yet sustained by a lasting weight and solidity. They are, in short, the reflections of those who have found the means to express themselves through architecture.

The elements in this book are the model I developed, a model not about rules and what you should and should not do but about people and their ability to put things together through ideas and imagination. It's a collection of stories from my own experiences and from those of the architects I interviewed. The elements are interdependent and simultaneous. Pull one and another must transform. They're infinite in potential, yet in order to describe the process, they are presented individually. Making small homes spacious, large homes intimate, modern spaces familiar and comfortable, crowded sites private, or sustainable design beautiful and cost-effective are just a few of the many challenges homebuilders face today. Based on both timeless principles and today's building methods, these elements should help you imagine a home that reflects your lifestyle and values, that successfully blends or contrasts different styles, that finds ways of reusing resources, and that guides you through daily activities.

This book is meant as a bridge between architect and homeowner. By facilitating an exchange of ideas that allows your home to take shape with its own personality and unique capabilities, I believe these elements will enable you to live the life you envision most strongly and hold most dear.

In a New York townhouse by Steven Harris Architects, a collection of art coexists with a collection of books.

Design Origins

Home is a vision, and this book is concerned with how to transform that vision into reality. There are few opportunities more meaningful and exciting than shaping the place where you will live. But arriving at a design that fully reflects what you've dreamed of building can be challenging. It often comes down to an exploration of your own personal sensibility, a quest to discover the origins of the designs that compel and delight you.

Consider the myriad influences on your sensibility over the years and through a variety of experiences. Here you will find the keys to your dream of creating the right home for yourself. The origin for your idea may be purely poetic, a memory of a place, for instance, softened and idealized by time. It's also likely that your dream will connect itself to one of the many other elements that provide a framework for home design—site, light, flow of space, lifestyle, or the environment—but at this early stage it's best to look into the core of an idea and try to articulate its intangible aspects before the tangible ones come into full play.

The inspiration for the Lake Muskoka Boathouse, designed by Shim-Sutcliffe Architects for a site two hours north of Toronto, included wooden boats built by local craftsmen and paintings by the Canadian artists known as the Group of Seven.

Countless conversations and changes will take place as a home develops. With the right kind of collaboration between architect and clients, the decisions will be guided by a central idea. The design, in simplest terms, is nothing more than a concept for building. During the development process, this core concept may be adhered to closely or deviated from on occasion, but it should always remain the logic behind the project. It is what will give your home its essence.

Unlocking Desire Creating a home begins with tapping into ideas and memories collected over a lifetime. Perhaps you've been inspired by the worn, textured stones you stepped on in an ancient city or by the dramatic way light fell across the living room walls in your childhood home. Perhaps you enjoyed the light, airy quality of a museum you visited or the way a friend's beach retreat seemed to open up onto the ocean. Maybe a children's story, a mathematical formula, or a report you read about sustainable living stirred your imagination.

Inspiration for a home can come from anywhere—travel, childhood experiences, or books (both reference and literary). It may be helpful to conjure up memories of beloved places by touring a lot of buildings, by looking around you at local, even

Symmetry, topography, and color all played roles in the making of Boxwood Farm in New Jersey, by Steven Harris Architects.

A rectangular reflecting pond enclosed by limestone garden walls ensures privacy for this Austin, Texas, residence by Gluckman Mayner Architects.

familiar design with sharper eyes. Start to pay attention to texture, form, and light. As you look at actual buildings or architectural images, encourage yourself to think precisely about what it is that you like about the space. Is it the mood? The symmetry (or lack thereof)? The materials or proportions of the room?

If you have chosen a site for your home, return to it and ask yourself why it resonates for you. Listen to it. Think about the winds that blow across it, the light that illumines it, the materials—trees, stones, water—that give it character. Do they have a strong enough presence to help shape the concept?

As you search for inspiration, remember: This is your home. While it may be important to you that it is in character with its neighborhood, tailor your home to your lifestyle. Take advantage of your individuality and that of your surroundings. Anonymity, that is, the absence of individuality in houses, kills a neighborhood with blandness. A well-designed, unique home, on the other hand, can inspire the community around it.

Communicating Your Ideas

Recently, I designed a Vermont home for a couple preparing to retire. Before entrusting their investment to somebody else, they spent months reading design magazines and books, thinking through their building priorities, and imagining ways to design around their lifestyle needs. This was a home the couple had been dreaming about for years, and they wanted to ensure that it fully reflected all of their ideas. When we first met, they had already generated dozens of specific thoughts. They wanted to build on one floor, orienting certain rooms toward the view; they wanted to be environmentally sensitive; and they wanted to be able to accommodate large family gatherings and their fondness for spending time outdoors. Affordability was also a key issue.

As they began the process of finding the right architect, however, they quickly discovered that each designer had a very different interpretation of their ideas. In fact, they likely could have created dozens of concepts, each distinct from the others and all based on the same ideas. Even when the concept had become clear to these clients, they needed to ask themselves: How do we effectively guide an architect through the intimate choices we've made during a lifetime of experiences?

You may not be used to talking about space, so sometimes it may be helpful to simply articulate what you want with phrases or a few adjectives you feel comfortable with. One client I worked with expressed her vision for a country home in Sonoma, California, with one word: freedom. We ended up designing a house with separate pavilions, each with very different enclosures and spaces, to allow a "journey" between places. Another client couple summed up their thinking with the word "strong," while at the same time saying that it was crucial that the house look "as if it had always been there"; those guiding ideas allowed me to begin work on the concept.

Communicating verbally has its limitations, of course. Unless you are an art critic, you know how difficult it can be to describe a painting; the feelings it evokes are sometimes beyond words. The same holds true for a design, especially since what you are designing will ultimately be built in three dimensions. So the more you can communicate in an architect's language, the easier the process.

To make the process more manageable, many architects suggest creating a visual sourcebook or reference folder. Most architect-client relationships, in fact, begin with the now almost mythic line "I want a place like this…," referring to a page in a shelter magazine or design book. If you've collected a series of these types of images, you'll be able to present clear ideas when you are ready to begin the design process. Tom Kligerman, a principal at the New York–based firm Ike Kligerman Barkley Architects, says that when his clients come in with images, they often don't think the pictures relate to each other at all, though invariably they do. "One way or another, you can pick up on the thread," Kligerman says.

When I meet with clients, I often present my own book of images to gauge the ideas they respond to. This works well because the photographs are vastly different from one another yet are within a range of ideas and vocabulary that resonates with me. As we talk, I collect the relevant ideas. After the meeting, I search for new images and materials until we agree on the tone and direction. While going through photographs, my clients for the Vermont house made clear their preference for local building traditions, and at the same time, they responded to photographs that showed more contemporary language. However, they seemed uneasy about choosing a few ideas rather than one "look." The next week, though, I received a letter from them with photographs of a highly glazed, white, minimalist, open-plan house in Los Angeles. The wife asked that the house include some of "that" in a few places if at all possible. We worked it out.

Keep up your visual sourcebook throughout the design process, collecting pictures of buildings and sites that inspire you. Continue poring over books, photo albums, magazines, and catalogs, and visit museums or antique shows for new ideas. Most architects would love to see a postcard that shows a painting or a piece of furniture you find inspiring. Sharing your thoughts in this way gives the architect an idea of materials or rhythms, and often he will be able to work the ideas into your project. This communication will make the house personal and unique.

Choosing an Architect
To arrive at a shared, collaborative vision, look for the architect interested in finding out what you want but still capable of bringing the depth of his own experience to the project. Says New York architect Richard Gluckman of Gluckman Mayner Architects: "One of the hardest things for an architect to do, but one of the first responsibilities, is to try to find out what the client is thinking, what the client wants, and what their expectations are, regardless of budget or program. Figuring out how to communicate with the client early and draw out of them what their real desires

15

When choosing your architect, take time to get to know not only his or her portfolio but also what he or she is interested in exploring. Although Ike Kligerman Barkley Architects is known as an expert in traditional design, this pool house on the New Jersey shore clearly has modern origins.

Peter Pennoyer Architects, another firm skilled in classical design, renovated a historic Virginia home with respect for the original architecture.

are—not what they imagine their desires to be—is critical. Some people imagine, well, we're going to have a new house, a new life, so we're going to cook more, or do more of that, and it isn't necessarily the case."

Many architects, in fact, liken part of their job to that of a psychiatrist, and it's not a stretch. In the first meeting, a good architect needs to find ways to get clients talking about some of the more intimate aspects of their lives. "The architect needs to try to discover not just how many bedrooms or bathrooms the clients want or what the budget is, but do they really want to go beyond a previous experience, or do they want something that is new but in some ways mimics or replicates their own experience," says Gluckman. "That is a challenge and a matter of early communication." Naturally, it's not critical that your architect be an amateur therapist, but rapport is important. You're going to spend a considerable amount of time with her, and ultimately, you want to be on the same path of discovery.

Once you've established that the collaborative relationship is right, look to the architect's portfolio. If you like the work you see in it—the proportions seem right, the rooms look comfortable—that's a good start. You can even bring a list of design issues and ask how the architect addressed each issue individually in her portfolio projects.

Philosophy is also important, so make sure to ask the architects how they approach design in general. Just because an architect has done a lot of work in a particular style doesn't mean she can't do anything else. As you evaluate the architects' portfolios and backgrounds, pay close attention to how they like to work. During these initial meetings, you should look for architects who are interviewing you as much as you are them.

If you're looking for a certain style, let's say a shingle-style, classical, or modern house, find an architect who likes working in that style and has the appropriate background to give you what you want. While some architects enjoy repeating historical styles, others don't like the idea of re-creating something from the past unless they're allowed to be inventive in the interpretation and free to infuse it with something current. Be honest about what you like and don't like, and ask whether the architect can integrate your ideas.

Asking an architect to work in an unfamiliar style can spur innovation, but make sure to place your ideas in the hands of somebody you believe will make them a reality. People often hire an architect not particularly suited to their needs. A "name brand" architect may have a signature look that is valuable as a work of art, but the finished house may not reflect your values. Ted Flato, of San Antonio's Lake/Flato Architects, describes three basic types of clients: the client who, in the interest of purchasing what she perceives to be a work of art, allows the architect to proceed unfettered, injecting few of her own ideas; the client who, in the interest of getting exactly what he wants, insists that an architect give him just that, even if it doesn't work; and the client who has clear ideas of what she wants but is willing to let the architect express them in an individualized creative vision. Asking yourself what kind of client you want to be may be the single most important question you pose during the design process.

Teamwork

Many professionals, not just architects, make the design come together. General contractors, landscape architects, interior designers, sustainability consultants, lighting designers, structural engineers, and a variety of other players can be crucial to the success of your home design. When you start adding up all of those fees, you might feel the expense is overwhelming. If you are working within a budget, a landscape architect, interior designer, or other consultant may not be feasible. If that's the case, you should make sure that you're working with an architect who is comfortable assuming some of those duties and that you're comfortable assuming the rest.

For critical issues, it's important that you have the right team, brought in at the right time. The key player will be the architect, and in most cases, it's her job to assemble the team. You should feel comfortable not only with her design ideas and philosophies but also with the people she can call on to help execute those ideas. Think of an architect as a film director, who needs to rely on cameramen, soundmen, editors, actors, screenwriters, and so on to create a distinctive vision. You need to assume the role of producer, taking care that you have hired the right person for the project you have in mind.

Visualizing the Design

After selecting an architect, you don't have to take it on faith that she has understood what you want. There are many tools the architect can use to illustrate what she's gleaned from your comments and how she's interpreted your ideas. For instance, architect Deborah Berke says that she and the architects she works with prefer to get out of the talking phase very quickly and put something more concrete on the table. Almost immediately, her studio begins to develop numerous

Architects' drawings can be invaluable in helping you to visualize a space. This elevation of a living room wall by Fairfax & Sammons is brought to life in the built space.

small-scale site models to study the volumes and the way they work with the site. Shortly afterward, the office begins to develop three-dimensional wire-frame computer drawings, continuing to update the plans, sections, and elevations as the concept comes into focus. Berke's studio, like many, works in a variety of media at the same time. Will you best "see" the design through a model, three-dimensional drawings, or simple architectural elevations, sections, and plans? Familiarize yourself with different types of models, and test yourself to understand what you do and don't see easily. Learning to read architects' language will help the design process, and after you've worked with your architect for a bit, you'll start to pick it up. Don't be shy if you don't understand the drawings. Always ask your architect to show you sections through the spaces and elevations as well as floor plans. Reading these will allow you to appreciate the spaces better than a floor plan alone.

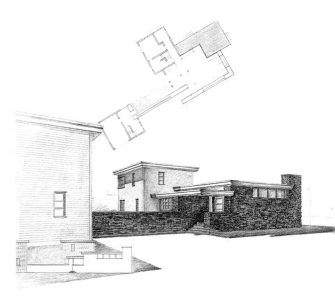

Even more helpful are three-dimensional drawings, site models, and large models of the interior spaces. Models offer a direct experience of the space—some of them you can even look into. (Of course, remember that you're at ground level, not in an airplane. Look at them from below, where you would be.)

Tom Kligerman is a big believer in the importance of models. He will build a model of the entire site, with all of its contours, and bring it out to the location. "It can be really crude; it can be made out of a clump of clay or a piece of cardboard, cut up," he says. "It doesn't even have to be the whole house. You can do one out of cardboard with just the basic shape, but it's worth the time."

Sometimes an architect will go as far as building platforms and full-scale walls with holes cut in them on the site so that he and the client visualize the actual views, scale of the rooms, and orientation. For one Ike Kligerman Barkley project, the information gained from a full-scale model changed the footprint of the

Rendering style varies from architect to architect. This single image by M. Finney Design and FARO Studio assembles a floor plan, an elevation, and a perspective drawing.

Some architects offer detailed renderings of interior spaces with fabric, furniture, and lighting, such as this representation of a Central Park penthouse by Barry Rice Architects.

house. Some clients hire a cherry-picker to lift them to the exact height of the view they want. Most people won't go to that extreme, and it's not necessary when understanding scale and siting issues can be as easy as staking out the house with a little twine.

Models and drawings are design tools for both client and architect. If a stairway seems too narrow or an area too dark, a model should show it. Seeing the design with the proper perspectives allows the client and architect to iron out any issues. Drawings and models take time, so be patient while the design develops. These tools are not only useful for you to look at; they are what the architect uses to think and create.

Honing and Developing Your Concept

A generating concept for a home is not unlike the concept for a novel, play, or song. It develops from the same sort of mysterious creative process, with surprises seeming to "appear" out of nowhere. From an intense study of the issues at hand, an order will gradually present itself. Over time (and with patience), many different ideas will intersect to create a concept that holds the design together and dictates the next move. "Once we discover the overarching order, then many questions are answered by listening to the order," says Los Angeles architect Steven Ehrlich.

"In a way, houses almost design themselves," Tom Kligerman agrees. "Once you know what the client's priorities are and you see the site, decision after decision falls into place." He says that when people tell him he did a great job designing a home, he thinks to himself that he didn't design it—he just took the information and put it together. "You just start drawing and it just starts to happen," he comments. Of course, you need to have a framework to encourage this sort of serendipity.

Whether or not lifestyle concerns are the big idea, I encourage you to place them near the top of your list. As you evaluate organizing ideas, think about what's most essential to you. What do you value, what drives you, and how do you want to live? Each of your lifestyle goals can be translated into a design idea. How can you make more time to read the novel that's been gathering dust on your bedside table? Design a comfortable reading nook for yourself. How can you make it easier to spend time with your family? Eliminate the wall between the kitchen and family room. And so on.

Maybe you have become aware of health issues relating to the way you've lived before and want your new home to encourage a more active lifestyle. The site of your home will influence this resolve, so if you haven't already picked a place, there are a host of important issues to think about. Can you walk or bicycle into town? Is there a park nearby? How will you get to your home most of the time? Can the children walk to school? Think about how sedentary your lifestyle will be if you always have to get in your car. Deciding where to live involves more than choosing a parcel of land. Your property is part of a community, and you should make sure to understand all of its dynamics.

Your Role In your search for the broader ideas that control the lesser ones, setting priorities is essential. How do you know what you absolutely need in your home? Designer and author Terence Conran suggests that when you go on vacation you take note of what you miss and what you can live without, then integrate these ideas into your lifestyle at home. It's an exercise in becoming aware of how you really want to live.

Great homes cannot happen without great clients. In every inspiring building, whether skyscraper, palace, church, or home, the patron or client who decides what is needed is as important to the process as the architects, craftsmen, and builders who

The trees on the site are drawn into this house on Orcas Island, Washington, designed by Cutler Anderson Architects, as a structural and sculptural element. This concept informs design decisions throughout the residence.

construct it. The best architect-client relationships are symbi-
otic. Clients willing to explore new ideas inevitably foster greater
freedom in the design process. At the same time, resistance can
be productive, pushing architects to think harder and invent
something they may not have considered on their own.

The chalkboard wainscoting and attenuated steel windows in this house in northern California by Fernau & Hartman are emblematic of the individualized home that will result from strong communication between you and your architect.

"The best clients are the ones who participate," architect
Larry Wente says. They recognize an opportunity to articulate
how they want to live. If they embrace that attitude, and hire a willing and capable architect, then the design process and even the construction hold great potential rewards.
"In the end, everybody is happy," Wente notes.

The most important thing clients need to know about the design process is that it *is* a process. And like any process, it involves change. Designs develop. You might begin with an initial concept, but that idea can easily take a turn in an unexpected direction. Perhaps the greatest virtues during the design phase are patience and flexibility. Odd as it may seem to include these as building blocks of design, they are, in fact, critical. Houses take time, and an additional few months in the design stage can mean the difference between a house that is merely functional and one that fully realizes your vision.

If you feel your architect is getting lost in the details, just remember that living room details can affect the way the room is framed or the design of a foundation. The structure of the roof can influence the space of the first floor or the basement. Your house is an integrated whole. You may feel that the contractor can pour the foundation while the architect is still sorting out roof issues, but it's worth working through everything before beginning construction. Because whether you move into your home in May or September, you'll be living there for years to come.

As in all creative processes, nothing should be set in stone—literally—until the whole work is finished. As Eudora Welty once wrote, "What its own author knows about a novel is flexible till the end; it changes as it goes." The same holds true for architecture. Don't expect a concept to stay the same from beginning to end. What an architect presents in the earliest stages is something like the outline of a book. Once the structure is designed, mechanical systems are planned, and ideas have had time to develop, the architect may propose an additional layer or twist to the core concept. This can be exciting. More often than not, the new idea offers a more elegant solution.

Developing a generating concept and creating a collaborative team will foster a shared vision for your home. To make that vision successful, you need to set the tone. The concept should not only give integrity to the greater design but also feed the process, resulting in a home that truly captures the essence of the site and the way you wish to live. Whether it's in the detailing of cabinetry or in the relationship of the house to the land, the concept you work out with your team should guide the process. In shaping ideas rather than styles or specific forms, a strong concept allows the process to be fluid and natural and, most important, to lead to exciting discoveries.

Bartlit Residence

Lake/Flato Architects

Architects David Lake and Ted Flato

say that when they first visited this textured, rugged site in Colorado that looks out to the Rocky Mountains, they had the same thought they often do when faced with building upon a beautiful landscape: "It's so wonderful without a house, how are we going to work with this?" The idea they devised in this case was to make as little visual impact upon the site as possible while heightening the experience of the land.

The house is set back from the crown of the hill, and when you first approach it from the street, you don't see a house at all. You see a series of walls and boulders, and you aren't aware of a building facade. Roof planes are covered in sod. "It's mysterious," says Flato. "It's not until you get right to the edge of the hill and start walking down the steps that the house comes alive." He comments that the house starts growing out of the hill, springing from the massive boulders on the site.

Organic, non-rectilinear walls connect these boulders, and you enter the house through some of these walls. The main circulation spine, which takes you from one pavilion to another, feels like an outdoor space because the floor material is the same stone you walked on outdoors. Enormous rolling glass doors, which slide into pockets when open, make you feel as if you are completely outdoors. The architectural materials connect you directly to the earth.

When you walk off those stone paths, however, you have a very different relationship to the landscape. You come upon open floating pavilions built of copper and steel that provide air, light, and expansive views to the mountains and back toward the hill that the house sits on. The contrast of experiences—the pavilions, the enclosed stone bedrooms, the intimate stone courtyards—reinforces and makes indelible the connection with the beautiful landscape around you.

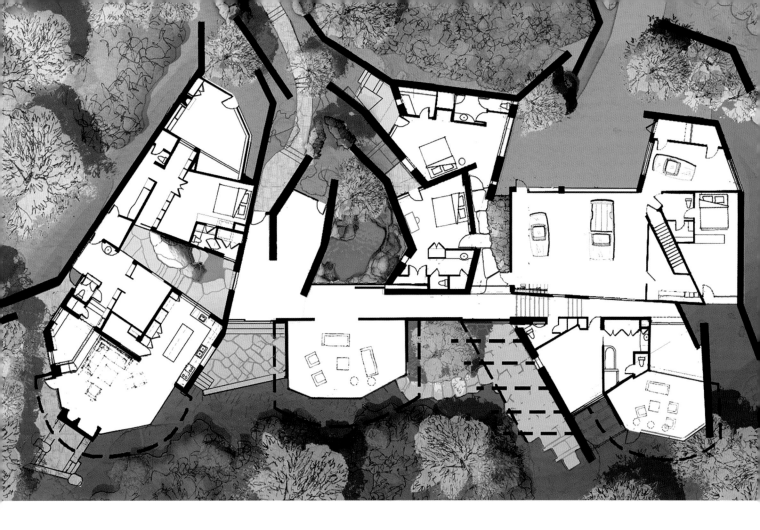

Site and Scale

Building a home transforms a site. Space is taken away, a house is added, and a parcel of land becomes a place. This can be either a positive or a negative event. In many areas of the country, beautiful old buildings, centuries-old shade trees, and native landscapes have been bulldozed to create the flat, treeless moonscape of contemporary suburbia.

It doesn't have to be this way. If we listen to the intrinsic values of the site, we can create structures that highlight nature's beauty in a wonderful way. New York architect Peggy Deamer cites the Golden Gate Bridge as an example. Her mother, who lived in the Bay Area before the bridge was built, told her that no one thought about that neck of water as the introduction to the San Francisco Bay. When the bridge was built, though, it suddenly created a dramatic entrance. "It's what you hope a building can do," Deamer says. "Not just draw attention away from something, but make it a place by making boundary lines, edges, connections, or thresholds."

A couple building on an island off the coast of Maine asked the architect, M. Finney Design and FARO Studio, for a house that would appear modest in scale, fitting in with the older structures on the island, yet would be large enough to accommodate the family's needs. Orienting the smallest facade of the house toward the water married these ideas.

If you view your site's native elements as building opportunities, not obstacles, the land will tell you how to connect with it. The crumbling barn can be demolished and carted off, or it can be reinvented and turned into an asset—a guest house, say, or a recreation room. The creek that splits the prime building space can be diverted or turned into a central element of the design. The brisk northern wind can be walled off or channeled into a natural ventilation system.

A house needs to engage the land, not just impose itself upon the surface. If you want to make a contribution to the land, the twin elements of site (the land and its features) and scale (the relationship of house to site) should shape your design choices from the very beginning. Whether you're building, renovating, or buying a home, you should be intimately familiar with all your site has to offer. Get to know the wind, views, sun and shade patterns, and other site features over time, at many different times of day and even with the changing seasons.

Visit and revisit the site. Like many architects, Cambridge, Massachusetts, architect Charles Rose tries to schedule every client meeting, including the first, at the site. You should ask your architect to return to the site with you as often as possible. The site inspires and helps make design decisions. And if you are not continually adjusting and fine-tuning the design to the site's individual character, it will be difficult to have your home contribute to the land. There are many methods that will maximize the contribution your home can make to the site.

Getting to Know Your Site
Think back to the time when you were shopping for a site, and consider what it was that you most wanted in the landscape that would surround your dream home. Did you long for trees, water, views, a wide-openness, or shifts in the terrain that would dramatize movement through the house? Chances are, this is the kind of site you ended up with. Now that the land is yours, keep sight of the idea that first attracted you as you walk through it. Those trees, for instance, are no longer an abstraction; they're a reality with all the wonderful idiosyncrasies that nature bestowed upon them. All the features of your site move from being types in your imagination to unique players in your home's design. Get to know them intimately and let them guide you.

You can orient your home on its site around considerations such as where you would like to dine, entertain, wake up, bathe, daydream, and drink your morning coffee. Rose says his firm thinks a lot about the connection of each activity to the site, and when you're walking your site, you should too. Think about both the big picture—how the sun rises, moves, and sets in relation to bedrooms or a dining room—and more individual concerns, such as how an outdoor shower and bathroom could be nestled in a gully. Outdoor activities are as important as indoor ones. Envisioning lounging beside a swimming pool, reading quietly in an Adirondack chair, playing croquet, sitting inside a screened porch, or eating outdoors helps shape interior spaces from the outside. Think about the interior and exterior simultaneously as you walk the site.

This residence in Orleans, Massachusetts, designed by Charles Rose Architects, was sited based on an intimate knowledge of the immediate area, including light and wind directions, views, and topography. Terracing provides a human scale to the landscape.

Having particular rooms relate to particular landscapes creates varieties of place, Rose says. Inside his Orleans House, which overlooks Cape Cod's Pleasant Bay in Massachusetts, the dining room has spectacular views of the water. Adjacent to the dining room on the inland side is the kitchen, which has more intimate views of the immediate landscape. In the interior courtyard, stairs lead up to the study, with its big, bold view across the bay, or down to the more inward-focused courtyard, which ushers you to the screened porch and the spa. The spa itself has an intimate relationship with

a vast landscape—the sky, which is subtly framed by roof forms. Each of these spaces has its own unique association with the outdoors, and sequenced differently, each would create a very different living experience.

The relationship between building and landscape can often be best understood in site models, such as this one of the Orleans House, which help develop ideas during the design process.

So as you walk your site, try to imagine activities inside the house and the relationship of one interior space to the next. A ball of twine to stake out interior and exterior layouts and a stepladder to understand second-story views may be useful. So, too, is a strong imagination. Pace the grounds until you can visualize how that stand of oak trees you'd thought of removing might just make a wonderful contribution to the view from your bedroom. Walking the land with his client provides important information to Tom Kligerman, of Ike Kligerman Barkley Architects, who describes the intuitive moment when they arrive at the appropriate place, look around, and know "this is it."

Other Ways to Get There
Any eureka moment comes after evaluating a variety of factors, including views, privacy (protection from the road or the neighbors), wind direction, and orientation to the sun. To show his clients how to observe these

factors and how the land moves, Charles Rose typically builds a topographic model of the site and, if possible, the area beyond. He and his clients then conduct what he calls an "imagery analysis," where they look at the different views the site offers, comprehending them in a clearer way. The client begins to see how, if he moves up the hill, the view will change. In this way, Rose and the clients are able to put together a three-dimensional catalog of views for a site. After many conversations with the client, he says, "We arrive at parts of the site that need to be acknowledged or celebrated. You want to build in response to them. We work from there." On a particularly beautiful site, there's an aspect of staying out of the way that is important, concurs New York architect Steven Harris. When he and his firm began to design a house on a spectacular site in Cabo San Lucas, the question of critical importance was how to avoid imposing the house on the site. The result was a residence that seems to have simply insinuated itself into the rocky landscape with an elegant inevitability.

In addition to topographic models, architects rely on site plans that show the site with property lines, salient features, and topography. Contour lines will appear on the plan at every foot or every five feet of change in elevation. If your site is in a subdivision, site plans should be available; if none are on record, you'll need to hire a surveyor.

You or your architect may also want to purchase a U.S. Geological Survey map, which gives topography and elevations above sea level for an entire area. When working with specific land elevations, it is possible to determine exactly what you'll see from which window, in what direction, and at what height with simple trigonometry and graphic studies.

Outside Forces

It is preferable to know what the buildable envelope (the allowable built volume of space) is before you buy a piece of land. Setback requirements, height limits, and any number of other stylistic restrictions will have a direct impact on the aesthetics of your building. Tom Kligerman says it is important to consult your architect, your realtor, your lawyer, and the local builder, because it is their business to know local building guidelines. For his part, architect Charles Rose says that his firm always investigates the zoning codes and other restrictions before his client has purchased the land. The architects then do small studies that help show the building envelope and what can be constructed within these limitations. Rose says his firm

likes the challenge of working within the confines of restrictions because sometimes they find an unexpected solution comes to the fore.

Architect Toshiko Mori raised this house one level above the land to better utilize the trees for shade and to allow panoramic views of the Gulf of Mexico.

A case in point is a home Rose and his firm designed in Chilmark, on Martha's Vineyard. Because the site is in a historic district, every new structure that exceeds thirteen feet in height must have a peaked roof. The code also dictates that houses have a shingled exterior and wood window frames that feature two panes over two panes. Yet by exploring the possibilities latent within the confines of the rules, Rose's house emerged with neither a peaked roof nor the typical windows but with an elegant, low profile that fit within the height restriction.

While it's best to buy a site that allows you to do what you want to do, it's not uncommon for people to acquire land (or at least fall in love with it) and then find out what's possible. If you learn that there are strict, traditional stylistic codes and you have your heart set on a home that doesn't seem to fit them, don't give up on your ideas until you've spoken with an architect. Sometimes it is possible to get a variance, especially if your architect is thoughtful and prepared when he goes before the building codes board, municipal authorities, or homeowners' association.

Tom Kligerman had the job of presenting the drawings for a home in Palm Beach to the committee in charge of approving projects in the town. His clients feared that the committee would not endorse the changes they wanted to make because they were not long-time residents of the area (they were from Michigan and had hired a New York architect). Nevertheless, their house passed on the first try due to Kligerman's sensitive design. Other architects and clients presenting that day were back for their second, third, and even sixth round of changes.

One aspect of Kligerman's success is his respect for the town in which he is building and its zoning board. A typical strategy of his firm is to sketch out a scheme that might not fit soundly within the restrictions and then find someone on the board to discuss it with informally. "It's much better to have these people working with you from the beginning rather than blindsiding them at a meeting with a huge presentation. People want to be helpful," says Kligerman.

Relating Climate and Comfort

As you get to know your site, remember that climate will play a role in the shape your home takes. A house relates the larger landscape to a human scale and creates a comfortable environment out of it. In rain, snow, or a sandstorm, or on a day with the perfect temperature, a home should be comfortable. That is to say, it should *appear* comfortable in the landscape outside and it should *be* comfortable inside.

Letting the natural elements participate in creating comfort enhances the experience of living in your house by connecting you to the land in subtle but profound ways. Nowadays, it is important that every building utilizes sustainable strategies. This no longer means thatched roofs or homes nestled under a berm of earth, though these are still valid ideas. Sustainability, above all, is about understanding how climate and comfort can work together. A good architect will always analyze your site, taking in all aspects of the climate that define it, particularly the prevailing breezes, sun angles,

*A desire to intertwine nature
and architecture influenced
this secluded glass
residence designed by
Toshiko Mori Architect.*

*A spectacular view guides
many spatial decisions during
the design process. Turner
Brooks Architect
took advantage of the
Vermont landscape in the
Yellow House.*

temperatures, and humidity. He or she may diagram sunlight orientation or wind patterns as a way of helping you understand the possibilities of the site. Air flow will suggest architectural arrangements of walls and windows to foster natural ventilation. It might indicate that windows on the northern side of a house should be minimal if cold air is an issue. A clear grasp of what your site offers prevents an overdependence on the systems you use in your house, especially air-conditioning and heating. What's more, sustainable architecture is not only environmentally correct but economically smart.

Scale Now you know your site in a physical, pragmatic way. And if your wanderings around it have been meaningful, you have begun to understand how to engage it. How do you want your structure to collaborate with it? Whether your home is geometric—rectangular or orthogonal, for example—multistoried in form, low and sculptural, or a combination of these elements, you need to have an idea for connecting the built structure to the land. Your thoughts will be expressed in the large scale and the organization of spaces on your site as well as in the smaller details of how building and landscape meet.

For a house built in the Utah desert, Peggy Deamer departed from her usual approach to the exterior surroundings by creating a house that excluded the land around it as much as possible. Indeed, she and her firm wanted to see the house "divorced from the land." The terrain in that area is very delicate, and the designers wanted the house to sit lightly on it. They weren't carving the land to accommodate the space. This didn't mean that it was easy to place, however. The resulting structure sits on a platform that rises above the land on one side and digs into the earth on the other because of a change in grade. Even so, the boundary between house and site is clear.

"This is about the house," says Deamer, pointing to the solid patio floor, and "this is about the land," indicating the sandy soil and shrubs. Creating a transition between the two was challenging; the area next to the house is part of the natural, indigenous landscape, but stepping from the porch directly into sagebrush would be abrupt. "It took a lot of dexterity to make the transition manicured, but still part of that landscape area," comments the architect.

By contrast, Charles Rose says that his houses are concerned primarily with the flow of space on the inside. He likes for a house to reveal itself in a gradual, fragmentary way.

43

"You can't stand back and see a Palladian villa, or symmetry," he says of his houses. On the contrary, you see forms that are sometimes enigmatic; you encounter parts of the house but not the whole. Rose places more importance on the experience of the architecture than on the objectivity of it. His approach has everything to do with the promenade—how you move up to the building, how you move through it.

Somewhere in between these approaches to the relationship of house to site is that of Steven Harris, who values the reciprocal association between his building and the landscape. For instance, his Boxwood Farm in New Jersey highlights the contrasts between structure and site. "At the site in New Jersey, there's this perfect plaid grass like Wimbledon," says Harris, "and a deep, rich, dark red floor inside. In some ways, it's the old Frank Lloyd Wright trick of making the inside the complementary color of what you're looking at outside because it makes the green greener to have a red foreground."

Distinguishing Far and Near
Looking out from the interior of a house, a viewer can have two distinct relationships with the site: an expansive one, taking in the vista in a broad way, or an intimate one, viewing features at very close range. Charles Rose, for instance, often relates the house to immediate features

From afar, Boxwood Farm in New Jersey by Steven Harris Architects presents a cluster of buildings within a large-scale landscape. One element that appears on a closer look is a fountain, itself an integral part of the site plan.

in the landscape, such as a tree, a glade, a potential courtyard, or an enclosed private garden. Then he tries to understand the house's distant views to see how the residence will frame or make a larger gesture to the longer outlook.

A house Rose's firm designed in Massachusetts makes his approach explicit: a beautiful maple tree stands in the middle of the site, and rather than take the tree down, he's building eight feet away from it. One of the rooms will be a "tree house room," he says. Tree branches will brush up against a glass wall, helping the branches and leaves contribute to the feel of the room. In winter, northern light will filter through the branches; in summer, the room will be awash in green light reflected off the leaves. In this way, the room not only frames the land but is close enough to have a sentient relationship with the tree.

In another area of the same house, a big pie-shaped corner of glass frames the distant landscape. A very long view passes diagonally through the site, beyond the yard, and across the undeveloped lot next door into a small grove of trees. Such a sliver view of the landscape animates the experience inside the house.

The Intimate Scale of the Body

In order for scale to play an important role throughout your house, it must engage the body as well as the site. The connection at this scale has as much to do with psychology as it does with architecture. Architect Turner Brooks is obsessed with the idea of nooks, recesses, and other places that you can occupy on a personal scale and that also relate to the larger scale. When sitting in a bay window, for example, your body is cozily housed in an alcove that also belongs to a larger room. As Brooks likes to point out, these intimate spaces are akin to the playhouses children make by covering overturned furniture with blankets. "Your body is snugly ensconced in a space within a space," he says. The niche or other small space forms a protective shell around your body, making the larger space outside more empathetically inhabitable. The layers may extend beyond the exterior walls of the house through landscaped areas, such as a lawn, and on out to engage the larger natural landscape beyond.

Spaces in a house can also engage the body as it moves. Although scale can be a difficult concept to grasp this way, it's easy to understand when you relate your choice of materials to the human scale. For example, we respond to alternating black and white marble floor tiles quite differently when they measure six by six inches than when they are eighteen by eighteen inches: the first acts as a field beneath our feet; the second contains our body rhythmically step by step. In this same way, rapid changes in materials engage us and draw our focus. When a small hallway of mahogany floors and concrete walls ends in an airy sitting nook surrounded by glass, the effect is startling and alluring. The hallway is relatively small in scale, while the nook, with glass walls extending to an impressive height, is quite the opposite—it invites you to sit down in the small place it has carved out.

Manipulating Site and Scale

"Here's the thing about all large houses," Tom Kligerman says. "People need two different kinds of space." In a very large house Kligerman's firm is designing, the

A small bridge in the Aquinnah House, on Martha's Vineyard, designed by Charles Rose Architects (formerly Thompson and Rose Architects), exemplifies the concept of relating to the human scale.

program calls for a dining room that can seat as many as 150 guests. The clients, who entertain the president of the United States, among other dignitaries, are perhaps unusual in some of their requirements, but like all clients they need a home that functions on a smaller scale for their day-to-day lives. With this in mind, Kligerman situated the dining room at the far end of the house; merely closing a door seems to make it disappear.

The other part of the house is where people really live. It doesn't matter whether your house is eight thousand or sixteen thousand square feet, people always end up in the little rooms, Kligerman asserts. This is true of a Palm Beach residence he designed.

Although the clients required very grand rooms for formal entertaining, they typically walk past the large rooms, with their numerous tall columns, to the family room. The room has a lower ceiling; the furniture is simpler and more comfortable. People seek out the family rooms, kitchens, and other small rooms in a house, as well as the little spaces, like libraries, window seats, and other nooks and crannies, that create intimate spaces within larger spaces.

Even though a home is large, it can still be inviting. Ike Kligerman Barkley's Palm Beach residence, in fact, achieves a welcoming demeanor from the street. Most people think it's a five-to-six-thousand-square-foot house, but it's actually eleven thousand square feet. All of the front rooms, including the dining room and the study, have low roofs; they and the connector to the garage are either one or one and a third stories. Even the garage, a two-story building, is not tall. By terracing the site a little and by making the ceilings very low, the architect diminished the house's scale. When you're on the second floor, you are actually in the eaves. Any tall structures, including the elevator tower, were moved to the back. It is when you see the house from the water that you can really grasp its size.

Creating Spaciousness
"An obvious trick for making the small house seem larger and more gracious," says Turner Brooks, "is to combine functions in an open plan so that the eye is invited to roam into areas much more expansive than those that the body actually occupies." Individual programmatic functions can be loosely defined within the larger field of space. Areas for living, dining, eating, and cooking, for example, can be combined, and these areas can be made still more generous by sharing space with hallways and stairways. In the houses he designs, Brooks likes to start with a box that, at a certain point, unhinges or unfolds to extend and expand the interior. He describes the quality of the space as stretched, taut, expansive. The ceiling may be shaped both to define the individual functions of a program and to lead the eye to visually participate in the adjoining spaces. The main area might open into another space that is a hallway or a bedroom on the second floor. A few columns may delineate a dining space or a lower ceiling may suggest a seating area. This kind of "borrowing" can take many forms. Where there are separate rooms rather than one large flowing interior, functions can be combined within a space and openings between areas can be large.

Another way that small houses can appear more spacious is through grand gestures and large-scaled details, says Brooks. "I've always admired how Greek Revival houses can be quite tiny and then have gigantic fascias, soffits, moldings, windows, or door frames, which change their scale from small to large," he notes. A little house that features a grand stair inside or outside, or a large porch that straddles the whole facade, feels bigger than its actual dimensions. Such elements add to a presence on the site.

Addressing Populated Sites

Typical urban site challenges include bringing natural light into large, open spaces and keeping out noise. When Charles Rose Architects inserted a new three-story penthouse behind the facade of a nineteenth-century warehouse in the Chelsea neighborhood of Manhattan, the designers considered themselves lucky that they could explore the factory then in the space in three dimensions. The architects gained a sense of the way light moved around the site and how the new construction might develop around it. They decided to make an expansive gesture toward outdoor space. To do that they had to assess the placement of the built areas in relation to that space. In order to have more exterior area, you need to be creative about interiors and smart about the amount of space you need. Rose used heavy masonry and triple-glazed windows to cope with noise on the site. "It's a remarkably quiet sanctuary," says the architect.

Suburban challenges are not dissimilar. People love spending time in their yards. Keep this in mind when you're looking for a home or building a new one. It's important to consider the amount of interior space you need to achieve a balanced relationship to the exterior. As our society grows and the amount of land stays fixed, the issue of both urban and suburban living takes on particular importance.

Though small in building footprint and modest in cost, this house in New Haven, Connecticut, designed by Turner Brooks Architect, presents a dynamic expanse of space.

Arrival, Departure, and Journey

How you arrive at and leave your site is how you begin and end the story you tell through your home. Some homes are approached and departed in a series of sequences; others have a more succinct progression.

Charles Rose often does multiple iterations of approaches to a residence when presenting schemes to a client. The various schemes each relate to and reveal something different about the site. Typically, there is an arrival sequence where a view is framed or a spatial moment is acknowledged. Rose addresses the moment of entry as well. Sometimes the architect sets up a foil, he says, as in the Chelsea penthouse. You enter the historic facade, travel up three flights of industrial stairs, and arrive at a little metal door at the top. You open the door and suddenly you're in an amazing garden. The low expectations belie the spectacular destination.

Urban sites offer a specific set of design challenges. However, as this garden courtyard in a New York penthouse designed by Charles Rose Architects demonstrates, they also present opportunities for inspired solutions.

It's not uncommon to see this kind of surprise approach to a house. Sometimes a long sequence through the landscape leads you to the house, and just as you get to the front door you capture a view for the first time—perhaps a stunning panorama of the ocean, a mountain range, or a beautiful yard. Other times, the entry is quieter, with the big views or grand spaces assembled like puzzle pieces, slowly and deliberately, until the picture comes together before you.

In planning dramatic or otherwise inspired arrivals and departures, care must be taken so that glimpses of parked cars don't interrupt the views of the site. In one Ike Kligerman Barkley house, a wall and an intimate garden are situated to hide parked cars from the views out dining room and gallery windows. The courtyard is directly in front of the house, but it's lowered. Steps lead up into the house, and then down again into the living room. The planting and elevation changes play down the courtyard.

Another home by the same architects features a driveway that winds around the side of the house—rather than a grand approach—so that the view from the door is of the lawn. An initial respect for the site instigated a decision that honored it. When the clients look out from their master bedroom, all they can see is lawn and beautiful trees. Arrivals and departures affect the main living spaces and beyond.

51

The entry sequence to this house in Seabeck, Washington, designed by Cutler Anderson Architects, skillfully choreographs the experience of the surrounding forest.

This stunning site in Nova Scotia required a particularly sensitive approach from Gluckman Mayner Architects. The residence is simultaneously strong in its design and gentle in its impact.

Canyon House

Steven Ehrlich Architects

If you've ever marveled at a set designer who effortlessly whisks his audience from scene to scene with a few cranks of a stage flywheel, you'll understand the clever sequencing central to Steven Ehrlich's Canyon House in Santa Monica, California. After you enter through a nearly hidden front portal, a subtle fusion of indoor and outdoor spaces unfolds through cutaway walls, flowing spaces, and views toward a series of cascading terraces, each one quietly inviting you to the next. "I don't necessarily reveal all of the wonders at once," says the architect. "I like it to be a discovery. Let the magic unfold, the magic of space, the magic of light. I like the notion that it takes time to get to know the house."

All of the main living spaces intersect in a complex spatial geometry that flows from one space to another and out onto exterior terraces through large sliding glass doors. The architect relies on a consistency of materials to ensure that the "journey," as he calls it, remains fluid. The materials—custom-colored stucco that derives from the bark of trees, copper, and wood—have their own natural colors, creating a seamless transition to the outdoors.

Outside, the journey culminates in a wide set of stairs that spills onto the back lawn. "I like architectural elements that are practical to also take on other meaning," Ehrlich says. "That stair could have been three feet wide, but instead it is a place for people to sit and becomes like amphitheater seating." As a designer, Ehrlich seeks to create "serene environments that replenish the soul." His Canyon House accomplishes precisely that by blending the familiar with the unexpected.

54

CANYON HOUSE: STEVEN EHRLICH ARCHITECTS

Chilmark House

Charles Rose Architects

To live in this house on Martha's

Vineyard is to immerse yourself in the landscape of the site. As you move through the house, you are continuously engaged with the surroundings, both visually and experientially.

The first way of describing this relationship is the actual, literal relationship you have with the land. Doors slide open to erase boundaries between the living room and terrace on days when the weather permits it. Intimate spaces such as a window seat frame a distant landscape view with transparent glazed corners, providing the illusion you are outdoors. Or a small jog in the full-height glass walls frames a portion of patio, bringing elements of the outdoors, whether rain, sun, or an animal that happens to wander close, inside. The topography of the land plays a role by inspiring the placement of volumes of spaces and views. The way you move up and down stairs tends to follow the contours of the land, as if you are outside when inside.

Another way to describe how the land engages you in this house is by painterly methods. Charles Rose notes that he and his firm often choose materials that play against the texture of the landscape, in this case one he likens to a Rousseau painting. The abstracted, clean wood and simple lines of the building contrast with and highlight the movement and shadows of the leaves.

Situating the inhabitants of this house in nature also involves a consideration of the intangible elements of landscape, the climate and the light. In the winter, the sunlight streams full force into the spaces, but in the summer it is very carefully screened through louvers and deep roof overhangs: you don't get any direct light into the house but rather a glowing ambient light. "The house is very peaceful because of that," says Rose.

FORMERLY: Thompson and Rose Architects

64

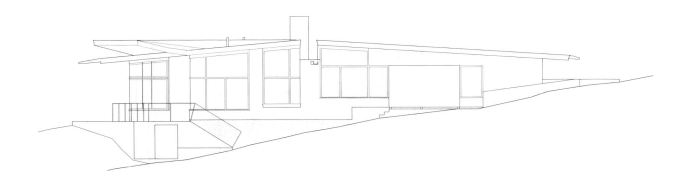

66

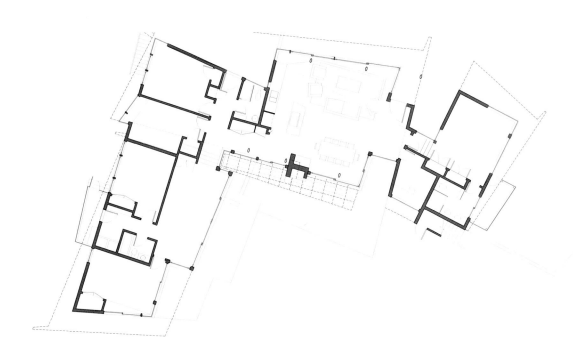

Serenity is the great and true antidote against anguish and fear, and today, more than ever, it is the architect's duty to make of it a permanent guest in the home, no matter how sumptuous or how humble. Throughout my work I have always strived to achieve serenity, but one must be on guard not to destroy it by the use of an indiscriminate palette.
Luis Barragán

We're such large dreamers here that we like to think we can make the client happy and the whole neighborhood happy, too.
Ted Flato

Language and Style

The style of a house is related to lifestyle. A traditional shingled farmhouse with wide-planked wood floors and distinct rooms offers one kind of lifestyle. A sculptural home with large glass walls and a flowing interior space offers another. New York architect Toshiko Mori says that sometimes people decide they'd like a modern home later in their lives after they've lived in or commissioned a more traditional house. They're familiar with one lifestyle and want to try something different. Other people know they want a home that is in keeping with regional materials and that makes sense in the area where they're building. They like the way that distinct rooms, even if they're sparely detailed, enclose space. Still others want classical proportions as part of something fresh and new. Whatever the specific requests, people are really talking about their values and the way they'd like to live.

Picking the language and materials for a home, then, is not just a "look." The choice is about values such as comfort, innovation, intimacy, quality craftsmanship, familiarity, economy, sensitivity to the environment, and logic. For centuries, architectural debates have addressed whether form follows function or function and form are separate, whether less is more or more is more, or whether

Stone houses in the Pyrenees of Spain inspired the stonework on both the exterior and interior of this residence in Montauk, New York, designed by Deamer + Phillips Architecture.

the goals are really "firmness, commodity, and delight," the formula proposed by Roman architect Vitruvius. These theories are all about the relationship of language to function and the value of language. In other words, whatever the theory, style is connected to larger ideas. Space and the materials you touch and see are about how you live every day. So the real question becomes: What language and materials are appropriate for you and your family, and for the climate and region in which you're building?

The Language of Architecture
Construction and details communicate a set of ideals and values through two different types of vocabularies. The spatial world speaks to our senses in an idiom of forces—heavy, light, soft, firm, easy, hard, in, on, under, above, and so on. Although expressed in a way we may not be aware of, the *language of spatial forces* is one that anyone can read. When passing beneath an archway of thick bricks, for example, we subconsciously think of the structure as weighty, even if we don't put that description to it. We "feel" a building material with our eyes and carry with us a vocabulary of these sensations. There are acute sensory differences between what it feels like to be underground, with light from above, and what it feels like to be in a glass room on a grassy meadow. More tangibly, a dark oak ceiling will feel heavier than the same ceiling painted white. The differences between the two can be understood with the language of spatial forces, which speaks to the feel of a building.

The other messages a building may communicate are the cultural expressions that have been handed down through time. These are a part of the *language of physical detailing,* and they involve the details specific to, say, French provincial, Federal, Greek Revival, High Modern, industrial, or an invented, blended language. Naturally, we borrow from other languages to create new ones, just as the Greeks and Romans building with stone borrowed methods developed for wood construction, and an architect designing a steel structure might borrow from the lines of a drawing.

When thinking about the language and materials of your home, the key is making sure that the physical language relates to the spatial, intuitive language. A pristinely modern apartment can create a warm, welcoming sense of purpose for its residents if the style innovations remain intuitively comprehensible. Detailing cannot be merely applied to a room. The scale and proportion need to make sense, and the spatial and cultural vocabularies need to be in sync.

Choosing the Language and Materials

The goal of architecture is a strong sense of place. "Architecture surrounds us and shelters us. It is the real world but it is also a vision," says Witold Rybczynski in *The Look of Architecture*. The space, mass, shapes, and materials must all reflect the same sensibility. Through ideas and instinctive choices, material language speaks to us. Style emerges from the decisions we make. Many language ideas come from the way the clients would like to live. For instance, even when the home is in a populated area, the residents may want the illusion of the countryside. Valuable clues may be found in the materials, proportions, and construction techniques of older structures in the area.

Modern in appearance yet infused with regional elements, this Connecticut home by Deamer + Phillips finds its own language. Materials with pared-down detailing coupled with bold forms hark back to local architectural styles.

The layout of buildings can be informal. Maybe the landscape is more wild than manicured. Or the clients say they'd like to live casually and close to the land. In that case, the architect may decide there should be no change of level from interior to exterior and, instead of a dense stone terrace, a patio of local stones, just the right size, detailed so that grass grows between them. The subtle transition between the meadow and the

The detailing, materials, and layout of this staircase in the Matchbox House by Gluckman Mayner Architects combine in a microcosm of the spatial experiences offered throughout the residence.

Metal components and nautical flooring evoke the feeling of a yacht in this kitchen in Westhampton, New York, by Ike Kligerman Barkley Architects.

terrace contributes to a natural and comfortable place to live.

Other style ideas are similarly subtle. They can be about the juxtaposition of refined surfaces against rough, unfinished ones or the balance of low-tech construction and high-tech construction; they can be about playing with expectations so that an element is familiar but has a fresh twist; or they can be about combining and recombining other languages to create something new. Peggy Deamer says that in a house she and her firm designed in Sherman, Connecticut, the clients knew exactly what they wanted. They asked for something unusual: a home with a contemporary exterior and a traditional interior. A stone floor of the sort that might be seen in Italy was one of the clients' particular requests; stone worked well with the ideas for the house because it appears old but at the same time may be designed to lend a modern quality. The clients did not want a flat roof, so Deamer and her firm developed a roof that was pitched but still appeared modern. Deamer's clients shared her predilection for open spaces abstract enough not to be language specific. How an architect articulates the thickness of a wall, making it look thin or deep, or divides a room with a screen, speaks to our bodies through spatial forces. An architect may use moldings, certain materials, and details, but these elements are secondary considerations. Space always speaks first.

Some language ideas are specific and storylike. Architect John Ike of Ike Kligerman Barkley Architects describes a nautical theme in one of the kitchens he has designed,

73

where metal backsplashes—inspired by something he saw in fashion designer Gianfranco Ferré's showroom—seemed to become seaworthy when riveted around the edges. Working with an auto body shop, Ike and his firm had the raw, riveted sheet-metal panels painted with car paint. The effect is smooth, shiny, and durable. On the floor, thin strips of maple alternating with wider strips of teak replicate a typical yacht deck. Cabinets of mahogany accented with painted wood are similar to those used in yacht construction. The exterior railing is of nautical stainless-steel cables. Even the lighting recalls ships—one lamp is actually made from a buoy.

It is important for clients and architects to discuss language early in the process, to make sure they're right for each other. While they are working together, they also have to teach each other their particular visual language in order to communicate effectively. John Ike's partner Joel Barkley tells the story of a client who expressed a desire for something "rustic." In Barkley's mind, this meant a material that was not polished, that had some weathering and patina, and that bore the marks of the hand that made it; something rustic could be made of a humble material. Ultimately, he learned that the clients had something else in mind. When he pointed at a drawing and used the word "rustic," he could see that they didn't understand. To the clients, rustic denoted the setting, not necessarily the material. What ensued was a conversation about the meaning of the word. The clients had something in mind more akin to a dwelling out of a Claude Lorrain pastoral landscape. This became clear when they showed Barkley an image of an ornamented, polished structure made of stone and stucco. Ultimately, the clients and architects continued the design process, finding different words to describe what each meant.

This kitchen by Gluckman Mayner Architects juxtaposes stainless-steel cabinets and streamlined detailing with a figural floor mosaic—a tradition dating back to the Roman Empire.

Color renderings or drawn perspectives help to avoid such misunderstandings. These, along with samples of the materials themselves, can convey an accurate picture of what the space will look like. Architects have libraries full of samples—wood, stone, tile, glass, metal—in their studios. A piece of barn timber, for instance, can say "rustic" in a quite literal way. Through conversations, materials, and drawings, the architect and client can be sure they're talking about the same ideas.

Developing a sense of ease with the language of architecture may be largely a matter of exposure to it. Peggy Deamer recalls a client who had many opportunities to review the way the finished project would look through models, perspectives, and exterior elevations. And yet, when the guest house of her residence was finished, she was surprised and dismayed by the look of the windows. She asked that the windows of the main house be changed before it was built. The scale of the window grids was colder and more modern than she had imagined. By the time the main house was complete, however, she had come to love the windows in the guest house. "Part of it is a certain comfort level," says Deamer.

Materials and Detailing
How do you know what materials to choose and where you can cut corners? Natural materials wear the best through time. Think of them as long-term investments. If you use the appropriate wood—mahogany or teak rather than pine for exteriors, for example—it wears very well. In fact, it wears much better than pressure-treated wood, though mahogany and teak are more expensive. Stone is more expensive than concrete, and glass is typically more expensive than plastic, though stone and glass will last longer. Setting up criteria for choosing materials helps to make decisions. When New York architect Richard Gluckman is choosing materials for a design, he asks himself, "How does this material compare to the original material?" and "What's the cost benefit?" The plastic he used on his own house may eventually fade, but it was so inexpensive that replacing it fifteen years down the road is still cost-effective. If Gluckman had built out of glass, detailing would have been much more expensive. He also knows that when he needs to replace the plastic, the materials available will be of a higher quality.

Even the highest-quality materials won't last forever, though. For example, wood shingle roofs, if applied correctly, can last fifty to sixty years. Metal roofs might last a hundred. Asphalt shingles have a fifteen-to-twenty-year warranty. For Gluckman, selecting materials is a question of what's appropriate. Dollar for dollar, for instance, you can't beat plastic laminate as a surface material. "As long as everyone goes in with their eyes open, people can do whatever they want," he says.

Yet it is important to keep in mind that some things go together and some don't. Choosing one language means that you may not be able to have something else. More often than not, however, you'll find that the most incongruent ideas can be combined in interesting, often beautiful, ways.

"For me, language starts with the structure of the building," says Richard Gluckman. Whether the building he's designing will be constructed of steel or of wood generates a certain approach to the subsequent materials. What you see in a building is attached to what you can't see, so the surface of a structure always hints at what's underneath. For instance, in a house Gluckman Mayner designed in Sagaponack on Long Island, which is constructed of lightweight steel, the experience of the steel siding and steel-and-glass window frames sets up a certain expectation of the other materials you may encounter. Naturally, the architect finds that the selection of windows and doors, and their material and construction, is crucial to how a house will look.

For Gluckman, language is not confined to the materials of the structure. For example, he believes that the choice of window treatments—whether the clients prefer Venetian blinds, draperies, or uncovered windows—is a fundamental language decision. He insists that the windows and doors of a building be selected early, not only for design reasons but for pragmatic reasons. He likens choosing the vocabulary, the system of operation, and the materials of doors and windows to deciding on the motor of a car.

Gluckman says that his studio brings in arrays of material combinations to consider. Architects in his firm may select two or three roof materials and two types of siding for the exterior, then sit down for a discussion. "If we select one material, it generates another response," Gluckman says. "It's not that you can pick one from column A, one from B, and one from C." Rather, the office has internal discussions about what these combinations mean and what they generate, as well as a discussion with the client on the conclusions. These conversations may set into motion the consideration of another kind of material. The team continues to work through the issues from the general to the particular, moving from the larger-scale elements to those of a smaller scale.

On the interior, Gluckman believes that flooring is the most important parameter for language. The sets of flooring materials for different spaces in the house, whether the living room, kitchen, bedrooms, or bathrooms, are established first and tend to generate the choices for cabinetry, ceilings, and so on. Not all materials work with one another. Sometimes clients will come to him and say, for instance, "We love the look of concrete." However, he doesn't like putting poured concrete in a wood-framed building, so he'll try to dissuade them. Gluckman believes that certain materials are conceptually compatible with other materials and some are not. In some cases, a client's strong predilection for a material or a jurisdictional requirement can generate the menu of materials. If the exterior must be shingles or masonry, that will generate the nature of the adjacent materials as well as door frames and, on occasion, even the structure of the building, according to Gluckman.

Borrowing Language, Blending Language

Architects create but they also borrow: from *everywhere*. Borrowing is different from copying. Buildings and details can act as models, precedents, and inspiration. Often, architects will look to many different sources at once, synthesizing what they see and transforming it into something uniquely their own.

Richard Gluckman has looked closely at spaces that appear in film and has also used industrial building and traditional Japanese construction as models for his work. He explains that it is important for architects to look at the work of other artists with the proviso that their influence is given due credit. He personally has gained knowledge of form, light, color, material, and craftsmanship from the artists Dan Flavin, Richard Serra, Jenny Holzer, James Turrell, and Bill Viola.

"It's hard to design without the possibility of quoting from somewhere or having someone make an association with something they've seen before," says Joel Barkley of Ike Kligerman Barkley. "Often, this is a lot of fun on a contemporary project. With classical detailing, it's a little different. Whenever you replicate a detail, it's interpreted differently." If, for instance, he looks at an image and tries to re-create a detail, perhaps the way stones are cut along the curve of an arch, he analyzes the picture carefully. But the translation is always off. The camera might be at a slight angle, and the detail he's working on is different. The detail always evolves into something different. At the same time,

the contractor might tell him how to change an element slightly so that it can accommodate something else. Classical architecture is always trying to resolve disparities that arise from difficult site conditions. "There is no such thing as copying things," Barkley says.

Languages don't have to be pure. A modern home can retain a comfortable feel; local materials and modern construction can be integrated into traditional styles; and classical choices can still leave room for surprise. A new house shouldn't seem like a museum of a particular style. "That's the fun of it, working with many different languages at once," says Joel Barkley. "It's weaving. To make architecture, someone weaves, knits, or pulls things together."

An architect communicates with different consultants, craftsmen, and the client to pull together something that's never been made before. When you assemble different influences, you have to somehow hold them all together. Architects need great skill and must work very hard to make the design cohesive. When a design is in the hands of someone who doesn't work at the synthesis or who isn't adequately skilled, the house ends up with dissonant languages that compete with one another.

Richard Gluckman remarks that an architect constantly appropriates or reexamines different methods of construction, whether historic or new, to blend them in various combinations. He brings up work his firm has done in the south of Spain, noting that an understanding of local building traditions is essential to his work there. A sensitivity to, say, stucco and stone can make a new building appropriate even if it uses the modern technologies of glazing and steel. "Almost everything has been done," Gluckman says. "We are constantly trying to reblend to come up with a new language."

Modern or Contemporary?
Modern means many things. It describes open, flowing spaces; it means sculptural forms; it speaks of pared-down, streamlined detailing. It is also a word that has been appropriated to refer to a specific period in architecture, roughly the 1920s through the middle years of the twentieth century, and to a later time that drew on the designs of that era, when such characteristics constituted a radical departure from the tradition of building. Using the adjective "contemporary" can sometimes be clearer, because it refers to the current time period.

Regional Maine construction and houses by Frank Lloyd Wright inspired the language of this residence by M. Finney Design and FARO Studio.

What looks like a modern house to one person might seem to another, particularly an architect, to be merely a building based on logic. Sometimes architects aren't even talking about language when they say "modern." They mean that the construction methods are up to date: fiberglass insulation, venting in the roof, and two-by-six stud-wall construction, for instance. Or they may be talking about the way people live, and the rooms and functions that are most often placed together. Make sure you and your architect are using the term "modern" in the same way.

Why think about a contemporary home? Choosing to design and build in a contemporary manner is optimistic, whether you ask for three-dimensional modeling of perspectives on the computer, build with an eye toward renewable resources, use new materials, simplify your lines, or opt for non-rectilinear, computer-generated forms. Whether you prefer homes that look like they were built a hundred years ago or homes on the cutting edge, remember that we live in the modern world. No matter the style of the house, we all want modern heating systems, plumbing, and ventilation. Older systems are obsolete or, at the least, inefficient. Larger windows, which were once prohibitively expensive, now bring light into our lives. New products and construction are not always better than old ones, but often they do represent improvements. Consider carefully when you're making your choices. It can be exciting to add something current.

Regional Ideas and Local Craft
You may hear your architect use the term "vernacular" to refer to the indigenous, regional construction of the area of your home. Why is this important? While there are no rules for what you should build, just as it makes sense to have some contemporary elements in your residence, it also makes sense to tie it to its community in a meaningful way. Where do you find regional ideas? Start by looking around you, and follow up with books that focus on your region. Your local architectural bookstore or nearby historical society will be able to help you as well. Often, regional ideas make sense for the climate and can save money in heating and cooling costs. Adapting ideas from old farmhouses or other solidly built structures unites the construction and language of your home with its community, strengthening a sense of place.

Taking advantage of local tradespeople also ensures quality craftsmanship. San Antonio architect Ted Flato of Lake/Flato Architects always keeps the local trades of an area in mind when designing. "If the area is famous for brickwork, or if there's a spot where the best trade is welding, or if there's a long tradition of masonry in the region, for instance, sometimes we can do remarkable things at a low cost," Flato says.

Roofscape, Ceilings, and Language

What's the relationship between roofs and style? A roof is about more than its looks and its ability to keep off rain and direct snow. While working out the spaces below a roof, architects consider how the roof will accommodate those spaces. It's always tricky to work out the roofscape. If you want two spaces to be adjacent to each other on the interior, you must think about whether it is a graceful move, or even possible, from the exterior. Depending on the type, roofs will intersect nicely in some configurations but will collide disastrously in others.

There are many kinds of roofs: gable, gambrel, pitched, flat, landscaped, and hipped, to name just the most common. All work well practically, but roofs are also capable of adding character to homes. You may want to consider a flat or low-pitched roof for your home. Although flat roofs are not right for every situation, they do allow for a different kind of interior allocation than other roofs. They can become roof decks or landscaped gardens. Traditional roofs often mean a traditional layout, with main, larger rooms on lower floors and bedrooms upstairs; a flatter roof or a shed roof can be more flexible. A living room can be upstairs, to capture a particular view, for instance. Flat roofs also allow very efficient construction. Whereas a pitched roof often requires dormers and many jogs in and out, a flat roof can just be raised to allow light to enter from all sides.

The stone wall ties this modern house by Lake/Flato Architects to its central Texas locale. The construction evokes stonework by the area's first settlers as well as formations found in the natural landscape.

81

People worry that flat roofs leak. It's a realistic concern if the details are wrong or the construction is faulty. The truth is that flat roofs are never perfectly flat—they need to be sloped to allow for drainage. When an architect designs the roof well and a builder knows how to construct and seal it, it should not let in water.

Another common concern is that flat roofs will store snow loads on top. However, as architect Peter Gluck comments, a low-rise roof can make sense in dry, cold regions because the roof holds only so much snow before it blows off. On the other hand, a pitched roof, with all of its angles, might hold as much as ten to fifteen feet of snow, loading the house asymmetrically. All of the snow slides off a steeply sloped roof at once; with a flat roof, structures can easily handle the weight.

Below the roof and inside the house, wall treatments and detailing where the floor meets the wall and the wall meets the ceiling give character to rooms. Ceilings, especially, represent a great opportunity to distinguish rooms with paneling, coffers, or beams, says architect Peter Pennoyer: "The wonderful thing about developing ceilings is that they are not furnished." Pennoyer likes designing curved, vaulted ceilings. In gabled roofs, he prefers to devise segmented vaults or coffered ceilings that allow you to connect the tie beams to the roof structure as part of the design. The vaulted and coffered ceilings make a room's identity stronger; even if you have huge openings into other rooms, you still know where you are, according to Pennoyer.

Precision in Construction and Detailing

Trim pieces and moldings cover joints in traditional construction. Baseboards conceal the joint between floor material and wall material while allowing for movement of the floor. Crown moldings hide the joint between walls and ceilings. Trim pieces also act as armor in a building: chair moldings around the room protect the walls from accidental bumps; casings around doorways protect the edges from wear. Traditional construction is about layering. The last layer is the most visible surface.

Minimalism works within a different philosophy. Compared with the simple detailing of traditional construction, it's an expensive way to build, demanding that the people who are working on the bones of the structure are as precise as the ones finishing it. In the construction of a traditional house, each trade covers up the work of the previous one. The foundation crew goes in first; the framer comes in and makes the

Essentially a collection of informally arranged, attached spaces with shed roofs, the Ridge House by Olson Sundberg Kundig Allen Architects animates the landscape as it nestles into its site.

foundation a little more precise; the drywall team covers up any flaws in the framing; finally, the finish team comes in with trim and paint and covers the flaws of the drywall team. In a traditional house, whether you pour a concrete foundation or build one of block, the precision of initial construction and dimensioning isn't as important as the craftsmanship of the finish work. But in a minimalist house that features exposed concrete, the concrete poured at the beginning of the project needs to be precise. You only get one chance in the minimalist house: it takes a higher level of commitment and more money to make a quality minimalist building.

Sometimes materials are put together in such a way that they are allowed to express their role in the construction of the house; other times, the materials are mute,

their roles, their very existences, are secrets vouchsafed only to the architect and the builders. Depending on what you're trying to say with the materials, either approach can be appropriate. Construction that speaks of its making gives a sense of human presence and often relates to the human scale. Think about a brick wall and the way you can imagine a person placing one brick on top of another on top of another. Bricks are easy to carry and are scaled to work by hand. Consider mottled stucco, where you can faintly make out the trowel marks on the surface, or wrought iron and its sinuous characteristics.

Architect Charles Rose often uses materials that show the evidence of their fabrication. In a house his firm has designed using copper, the metal is being installed by hand to give it a crafted sensibility. The effect is intentionally not clean or crisp, as it is when large, machined panels are used. For Richard Gluckman, who frequently uses prefabricated cementboard, the expression of the fasteners is still important. The panels can be mounted without expressing their

A natural wood-planked ceiling and rafters contribute to the cozy feel of this Fire Island beach cottage by Peter Pennoyer Architects. A flat, painted ceiling would have produced a considerably different effect.

construction, but because they are thin and not solid concrete, he thinks they should look like what they are—veneer. The method of construction is apparent.

On the other hand, the absence of the maker's hand can have a scaleless, monumental, sleek, or serene feeling. Certain seamless surfaces show no joints, no fasteners, no marks. The fasteners are invisible. When you cannot see how something is made, it often has a mysterious quality.

Compare and Contrast

Contrasting materials—rough against smooth, luminous within earthy—calls attention to them in ways that heighten their particular characters. The contrast speaks to us. Architect Richard Gluckman likes to combine inexpensive and rich materials. For instance, he uses cementboard in combination with high-quality stone or back-painted glass, and materials like solid surface and plastic laminate in combination with richer materials. Careful detailing gives the inexpensive materials a high-end look. He also uses expensive materials detailed in a simple way.

Architect Steven Ehrlich also designs with contrasting materials. In his own home, he has created a counterpoint between the "primitive" and the "future." He describes the sixteen-foot-long, sandblasted concrete-block wall in the living room as "the essence of wall." It is also a fireplace. Perpendicular to this wall, at each end of the room, are large sheets of glass, fifteen feet wide by sixteen feet high; these pieces of glass can completely slide into a pocket in the wall. "Technology allows us to build these glass doors that literally slide away and evaporate," Ehrlich says.

Peggy Deamer contrasts heavy or thick materials with lighter or thinner ones. She may detail a thick wall so that it appears lighter or contrast a stone wall with a thin metal roof. The contrast works well in details, but it is even stronger when it's carried through an entire project.

Distant Language and Near Language

Inside a house, the scale of materials has to become refined and intimate, more appropriate to the human body than to the landscape. People experience materials of a building differently depending on how close they stand, and an architect takes this into consideration in her designs. From a distance, the scale of a building responds to the larger site. You see the volumes and voids and changes of materials more than the details. Shingles appear as a finely

85

dappled surface; stucco gives the impression of a uniform plane; and a glass curtain wall reflects its surroundings or glows with light from the interior. Up close, the materials appear as they are detailed. There is the possibility of touching them. In a Texas house, Richard Gluckman's firm used very large precast panels on the exterior; inside, much smaller, cut stone was used. "The transition between large- and small-scale takes practice," says Gluckman.

How the house is perceived in the landscape can help make decisions about the exterior materials. The color of the earth and the bark of trees, the character of foliage, snowy hills, a meadow, or a yard of grass become part of the palette, along with the materials of your house. Mexican architect Ricardo Legorreta collected stone from the Sangre de Cristo mountain range in New Mexico that ultimately influenced the colors of the Visual Arts Center he designed for the College of Santa Fe. The possibilities for inspiration are as varied as the landscapes around us. From humble stone to white sails—grandly mimicked by Jørn Utzon in the Sydney Opera House—the clues for interesting design are there for the taking.

What Makes A Design Endure? You should want to embrace a building.

It should engage and invite you with its materials. "Whenever you come in contact with the building, it is a very pleasing, sensual experience," says Charles Rose of a house he designed in Cape Cod, Massachusetts. If he's making a groove as a handle for a sliding door, for instance, he thinks about how it feels; he considers optimal comfort and ease of use. One strategy he uses when designing furniture for his projects is to differentiate between parts of the furniture that you touch and parts of the furniture that you see. "We're more high-touch than high-tech," he says.

Joel Barkley adds that anything within reach should be sumptuous and wonderful to touch. You can accomplish this by paying close attention to the feel of doorknobs and drawer pulls, or to the material of the bathtub, he says. All of the senses are important in design. Even the sense of smell can come into play when choosing materials, for both indoors and out. The scent of eucalyptus trees, herbs, pine wood, or cedar boards adds yet another dimension to the design of a place.

Fireplaces are not simply functional. A fireplace in the Ravine Guest House in Toronto, designed by Shim-Sutcliffe Architects, is a focal point that informs the language of the surrounding space.

Certain buildings draw people back to study them again and again. Sometimes they're very simple buildings, sometimes they're complicated. "Certain things are studied no matter what is going on stylistically," says Barkley, who cites the seventeenth-century Villa Rotonda, designed by Andrea Palladio, as an example. There is something there beyond style that speaks to different ages, he says. Frank Lloyd Wright's house Fallingwater is another seminal house. Its open space, horizontal windows, and cantilevered balconies speak about larger ideas in the world. These buildings ask philosophical, existential questions through their spaces.

The simple detailing and limited material palette on the interior of this East Hampton, New York, residence designed by Deborah Berke & Partners create a smooth transition to the exterior.

Yet classic wooden farmhouses also endure, as do regional stone houses and well-conceived houses of every language. Over the three or four millennia humankind has been building, fundamental qualities consistently rise to the fore, such as scale, proportion, natural light, and materiality. Common threads run through both the wood and paper of the humble Japanese house and the cut stone of an elegant palace. Each in its own way is appropriate. And as Richard Gluckman is wont to say, "Appropriateness endures."

*Sinuous wrought-iron
railings and hand-painted
tiles and ceiling mark this
San Francisco house by Peter
Pennoyer Architects with the
character of an artisan.*

Diamond A Ranch

Peter Pennoyer Architects

Architect Peter Pennoyer says that

renovating and designing this ranch in New Mexico was both interesting and challenging because it was large, spread out, and embodied many different styles. The buildings needed to be completely reconfigured and reinvented. "What was wonderful about this project was that it was an opportunity to explore different periods in the local history of the local architecture on the Santa Fe trail," says Pennoyer.

Existing on the site were rooms that were created within a rebuilt nineteenth-century stagecoach inn with rough surfaces and packed dirt floors; areas with primitively constructed Greek Revival details; a library, which looks more like a ballroom, with Irish oak paneling and a sixteenth-century mantelpiece; 1950s concrete-block additions with small windows; and a Bauhaus chapel that was designed in the 1960s on the grass opposite the house. Even the chapel incorporates older fragments of ruined Mexican churches.

The idea of the design was to create a fictional history for the place through time. Pennoyer says that he created a narrative in his mind about making courtyard, library, bar, dining room, and various other rooms feel like they are part of the story of the evolution of the house. None of them feels too different; you can imagine that they grew over a hundred years instead of having been invented all at once.

INTERIOR DESIGN: Thomas Jayne Studio

Only connect.
E. M. Forster

Like a musician's breath to a wind instrument or touch to a percussion instrument, light and shadow bring out the rich qualities of materials which remain mute and silent in darkness.
Steven Holl

Openings and Light

At its most basic, a house is about the relationship between an interior and an exterior world. The exterior is exposed to the elements—light, rainstorms, humidity, or snow—and open to the road, the neighbors, perhaps a town center or a forest. The interior can be vastly different, a small world of its own; at the opposite extreme, it can pull the outdoors in and go out to meet it. Homes are introverts or extroverts in the way they open up to or close off the world around them. Present or absent, modulated or freely flowing, light animates space, presents views, and sets a tone through its intensity and depth. The number and character of openings in a structure can expand your experience of a home, protect you, expose you, delight you, and even guide you through its spaces as you go about your days.

Though intangible, light is an architectural material just as are the walls, floors, ceilings, and land upon which the house sits. Learning how to work with it is similar to learning how to manipulate other materials, with a few key differences: no other material is by its very nature so immaterial and changeable, even capricious. And no other material requires a partner to give it substance. Openings perform that role for light, so the two are inextricably linked. Because you have to think about openings

In the Ravine Guest House in Toronto by Shim-Sutcliffe Architects, large glazed doors fold away so that interior and exterior spaces merge seamlessly.

and light simultaneously, any consideration that involves them cannot be separated from the design of space. Light can come into a space in layers from above or from behind a wall so that it gradually reveals itself to you; it highlights something spatial, a moment of circulation. Or the opening may be the glass wall itself. Proportions of an opening as well as materials, details, and placements create various qualities of light. You can design punctuations of light; you can frame light; you can bring a window to the edge of a wall or ceiling plane so it washes the surface with light. Clear glass allows vision, while other translucent materials choreograph vision, allowing you to see only shadows and movement in the distance. Stained-glass windows placed carefully can throw unexpected colors across a room. Depending on the design, light can be modeled, captured, reflected, refracted, transmitted, colored, focused, or diffused.

As in a work of art, there is a compositional quality to light as it relates to rhythm, proportion, layering, and depth in spaces. Too much light can be as bad for a space as too little. Various enclosures and levels of interior and exterior interactions rely on the precise quality of light for their beauty and contribution to the home. How light connects our daily activities, how its changes chart the progress of a day, how the openings that reveal it show us the world around us or edit out unwanted views—these, and myriad other aspects of light, make it a vital part of your home.

The Basics Natural light is always changing. Moment by moment, there are infinitesimal variations as the sun moves across the sky, so that the light in a room at two different times of day, or on two different days, is never the same. We enjoy these variations. The quality of light—its subtleties of tone, intensity, and color—can be more important than the quantity of light.

To better understand the attributes of light and how to design with them, it helps to recognize three properties. Light can be transmitted, reflected, or diffused through the material it enters. Transmission takes place when light passes through a material such as glass; think of translucent glass. When light bounces off a material, we call it reflection; think of glass with a mirrored surface. When some or all of the light is captured within the material itself, diffusion takes place; think of very thick or cast glass. Often, when light enters a material, two or three of these properties are in action, not just one. As light enters your home through a glazed opening, most of it is transmitted to the

Light reflecting upon walls and other materials inspires surface compositions such as this pool enclosure in the Winter House by Ibarra Rosano Design Architects.

interior, but some will be reflected off the surface. With sandblasted glass, some of the light is transmitted and some is diffused; the diffusion makes the material appear to glow.

Differing qualities of light affect the way we perceive space and materials. Bright, direct light will imbue a white oak floor with warmer tones, while indirect light can suffuse a stark white room with an inviting glow. A room painted in a dark, rich gloss comes alive in dimmed light or candlelight.

Openings are more than just windows and doors. An opening may be a skylight or light well, a cupola, a thick stone or concrete archway, a tall space with an open balcony above, or glazed walls that allow light in from many sides. I find it useful to think of openings not as windows and doors but in terms of spatial perceptions and views. You can consider traits of light, heavy, solid, and void.

It helps to imagine what you will see from inside the spaces across one room into another, as you walk up a staircase, from inside the house past an outdoor courtyard, or as you approach the building from the outside. You might imagine going from a darker, heavier space into a lighter, brighter one or vice versa. During the design process, these vague notions become more concrete. At the beginning, something you think of as a void might actually become a mirror, reflecting light from across a room. Or perhaps it might develop into a window wrapped around a corner, allowing an uninterrupted view in an unexpected direction. Or it could turn into an interior window that carries light from the outside through two separate rooms.

Openings are about moments and transitions, but they also need to make sense in the overall experience of a home. Openings place you in the world, and in a sense, you want to tell a story with that placement. For a home designed so you are living low to the land, with screened porches all around, there's an easy transition between indoors and out. The center of the home, constructed of thick stone walls, is a protected space, while the porchlike rooms are basically outside with a sheltering roof. There is a consistent, clear idea of the relationship of interior to exterior throughout the house.

Clerestory windows, large punched openings, and multiple entries animate the living room of this residence in Orleans, Massachusetts, by Charles Rose Architects.

Daily Activities and Changing Light

For architect Ted Flato and his firm, Lake/Flato Architects, the overriding issue in beginning the design of any house is connecting the house to the light of the sun. "We have an enormous desire for people to be aware of the changing time of day, the way the sun grazes a particular wall, or the way people move around and use a house with the changing light," he says. It's important to explore your ideas about light. Then you can begin to understand what should be solid versus what should be light and airy. If a client wants a darker bedroom or a bright kitchen, for instance, this informs the design.

It's crucial, then, to discover and articulate your ideas about light. Think of spaces and activities in terms of qualities of light and times of day. Do you like to wake up with the morning sun streaming in your windows, or are you a late sleeper? Where do you want the most light during the middle of the day? Where will you read—in the library or in your living room—and at what time of day? Where will your computer be and what kind of light is best for your work? Are there stars in the sky in the evening that you might be able to see indoors? Can you view the sunset from your house? While a sunset can be mesmerizing, equally as powerful is the view of a warm, glowing landscape lit by the setting sun. A dinner table can make use of that view, while an area for cocktails or relaxing could face the sunset, or vice versa. Often, people prefer morning light in kitchens and breakfast rooms so that they wake up to the light; there is a valid argument for southern or northern light in kitchens as well.

While you're thinking about your home as a whole, let the path of the sun help you arrange both indoor and outdoor spaces on the site. When I'm in the early stages of design on a project, I turn out the lights, light a lamp or candle, and move it over the site model in the path of the sun. This helps to make decisions about where to place terraces and specific rooms and gives me a better idea of what should be solid and what should be open to the light. This exercise helps clients imagine which rooms will receive morning sun and which will get daytime sun, as well as understand where the sun sets in the various seasons. This type of site model must be large enough in scale—at least one-half inch in the model to one foot in real space—that you will be able to view the light accurately. But as a study model, it can be made simply from chipboard; time-intensive details aren't necessary.

Following the Compass Knowing key concepts about the relationship between light, openings, and the basic compass orientations will help significantly in making the leap from ideas to reality. We all know that, relative to where we are, the sun rises in the east, heads toward the south, and sets in the west, and that, depending on the latitude where we are building, the angle of the sun will vary in the sky. In the winter months, the path of the sun is lower in the sky, and it is at its lowest point on the winter solstice; in the summer, the sun travels along a higher path, and it is at its zenith on the summer solstice. What does this mean for openings and light in your home?

In early morning and late afternoon, the sun is low in the sky. At this time, there is a greater chance of glare because light can come into windows directly toward you. Glare is the effect of extreme contrasts of light, and it strains the eyes. If you're planning to use

104

A continuous strip of Profilit glass surrounds the perimeter of Shim-Sutcliffe's Ravine Guest House, capturing light from all directions.

an east- or west-facing room as a study, you can provide screening or light shelves (horizontal surfaces that reflect light upward). Heat gain from light is also a concern, especially in west-facing rooms, because temperatures are generally higher in the afternoon than in the morning.

The sun shines most of the day from the south, and there is greater variation in the sun angles from that direction from season to season. The placement of openings can allow warm light from the lower winter arc of the sun to enter a home, while overhead shading devices can protect from direct light when the summer sun is higher in the sky.

Northern light does not mean darkness, though. Northern light is, in fact, the most constant light. It's also diffuse, sometimes intensified by reflections from the ground outside, from trees, or from nearby buildings. Artists and craftspeople prefer northern light because of its evenness and consistent color rendering. I recently designed a kitchen with a north-facing, eight-foot-long-by-four-foot-high window above the sink and countertops. The client was nervous that there wouldn't be enough light, but in fact, the north light is plentiful. In most climates, fewer and/or smaller windows are placed at the north (south in the Southern Hemisphere) to cut down on heat loss. In cold climates, service rooms such as closets, bathrooms, and mudrooms placed on the north side can act as insulating barriers.

One of the most important pieces of information about the compass points and the sun is that magnetic north and true north are rarely the same. Magnetic north refers to the northern site where the geomagnetic field points vertically, while true north refers to the geographic North Pole, where all longitude lines meet. On your site plan, the large arrow that points north usually indicates magnetic north. You or your architect need to look up on a chart how many degrees east or west of magnetic north true north lies. The sun follows a path designated by true north, and so the corresponding eastern, southern, and western directions on the site plan will vary from the actual path of the sun. The sun rises at true east, not magnetic east, and it sets at true west, not magnetic west. It's worth the few extra minutes it takes to calculate the true directions.

Once the spaces—the solids and voids—begin to develop, you can draw sun diagrams that will tell you exactly how much sun will enter a space on a specific day and time. If you'd like to know whether you'll have sunshine on your pool terrace at six in the evening on the Fourth of July, you can figure it out.

Wind direction and velocity, humidity, and temperature also play important roles in positioning a house with regard to its openings and the compass points. Your architect should be intimately aware of the climate and how materials and openings can heat and cool homes naturally.

A Palette of Possibilities
If openings and light are architectural materials that encourage various psychological and phenomenological states, then those who design homes should be mindful of the many, often subtle, ways they work. Some spaces glow with light. They're illuminated by the sun and there's never glare. The light is diffuse and soft. An architect can achieve this by planning for indirect and reflected light. Thinking about the height of the ceiling, the distance of the walls from the windows, and the proportions between these and the height of the windows is part of the process. Tall windows in a shallow space with high ceilings, for example, allow light to enter and reflect off the opposite walls, floors, and ceiling. Loft spaces often have this kind of light. Directional skylights can achieve this, as can other light wells and layering of walls. The noted Finnish architect Alvar Aalto invented light systems that washed southern light downward onto northern wall surfaces. Especially in the northern latitudes of countries like Finland, where light shines only a few hours a day in the wintertime, capturing all potential light is a necessary challenge.

Materials that hold, reflect, and transmit light are varied. Glass—the material we are most accustomed to seeing in buildings—can be bent, cast, sandblasted, laminated, beveled, or colored. Plastics and other materials can be laminated between glass layers; microscopic louvers can be integrated into glass to direct vision and light; and glass can be painted a color or a metallic tone with a very clean finish. Architectural glass is commonly plate glass, whether single-, double-, or triple-pane, and there are many finishes available for sun protection. In addition to glass, acrylics, fiberglass products, and even glass-embedded concrete, as well as metal screens and other materials that can be woven or perforated, may be used.

Year after year there are many innovations and technological developments in glass, including glass with higher insulating values, greater tensile strength, and photovoltaic capabilities. The skin of a building can actually gather energy and direct it where it is most needed. Structurally, glass can be used in ways it never has been before, supporting more weight and spanning greater distances; a once precious membrane has become an important building material. It's important to be open to how these innovations can be used in buildings, including homes.

Shading Devices

Screening or filtering bright light can be important. At a house Charles Rose Architects designed in Chilmark, which is situated on a sloped promontory that overlooks what he calls Rousseau-like woods, the sunlight streams in "full force" in winter, but in summer it's carefully screened through trees or through louvers on the south and west windows. Deep overhangs further ensure that direct summer sunlight does not enter the house. Rose says that the house has a noteworthy quality of ambient light indoors: "It just glows all day."

White surfaces capture the daylight and emit a diffuse glow in this breakfast area of an East Hampton, New York, house by Deborah Berke & Partners.

Along with deciduous trees that filter sunlight during summer months and allow it in during winter months, mechanical and fabric shading devices help do the trick. Peter Pennoyer says that a pocket in the ceiling allows window shades to disappear. The pocket can be constructed to accommodate two types of shades: a solar screen and a blackout screen. In combination, these provide almost absolute control of the light level. When the architect provides a pocket for the shades early in the design process, they can be built in without covering the architecture. Lorcan O'Herlihy uses a similar concept in his Lexton MacCarthy House. Two sets of curtains—curtains with a reflective silvery background in front and fabric panels in back—hang in this residence.

It's easier to control sun from the south than from the east or west. As Richard Gluckman says, there's "a narrower range above the horizon, even over the course of

107

a year, than with east or west orientation, so a very simple horizontal screen will keep the sun off south-facing glass." Many architects plan for screening devices to mitigate damage from harsh summer sun. For large glass walls and doors in his own home, Steven Ehrlich attached big canvas shades, which can be raised and lowered by remote control, to an exterior steel frame.

Peter Gluck, on the other hand, considers curtains a problem. In traditional houses, he says, "They close up the glass." The outside of a house he designed in Chicago is constructed of sandblasted, translucent glass specifically to avoid curtains. In Aspen, where Gluck has designed houses in the middle of the town, he steered clear of curtains by putting living rooms on the top floors where "you don't see the activity from the street, and you have mountain views all around."

Openings and Experience
Views in a house are so important that, together with a few other pieces of information from a client, they may dictate the basic layout and character of a residence. It's important that views are varied. No matter how gorgeous a mountain range, it loses some of its drama if every room in the house presents the same panorama. Options for providing views are endless. You can frame them, allow them to be fully uninterrupted, or create suspense by slowly allowing glimpses of what's ahead. There should be an idea behind the way the home reveals views as you walk through the space.

Southern views are the easiest to work with because they have the most sun. Naturally, you want a fair number of windows where the sun shines and where the view is, so there's no conflict between seeing out and allowing light in. Northern exposures, however, can sometimes be problematic. Tom Kligerman of Ike Kligerman Barkley designed a house in Michigan overlooking a lake to the north. In this case, he wanted large windows on the north side, but northern light is cold and blue and he wanted something warmer. He opened up the house so that the main living room passes all the way through it. A very large picture window on the south wall invites warm southern light into the entire room. The window looking out to the lake is relieved of its lighting duties.

Sometimes we want light without being able to see outdoors, perhaps because there are other houses or unpleasant sights in a particular direction. But this doesn't mean we can't have natural light in the room. In many cases, it is possible to bring light in from above with a glass ceiling or skylight or a band of clerestory windows high in the room; we might also choose an acid-etched or other translucent glass.

O'Herlihy's Lexton MacCarthy House faces Hollywood, and large openings in the front of the structure frame those views. On the sides, where the view is of other houses, he used clerestory lighting and invented a wall system for admitting light without views. The wall is pulled away so that the one-by-six pine siding is visible as it goes past the glass; half-inch gaps between the siding slats allow light to filter through. The idea is in keeping with the siding system for the whole house: one-by-six pine siding "floats" away from the building to help it breathe and provide waterproofing.

Slender steel columns and minimal door and window frames lend this residence by Toshiko Mori Architect an immediate relationship to the surrounding nature.

Artificial Lighting

For gray days, evenings, and times when we're awake late, we need light from lamps to be as inviting and variable as natural light. We also need lamps as supplemental lighting when natural light is not strong enough.

109

Lamplight is an architectural material, just as natural light is, and there should be a balance between the two. Use dimmer switches wherever possible so that light conditions can be adjusted. Think about layering lamplight, so that during any activity or any time of day there is appropriate lighting. One layer might be general or ambient light, which provides a uniform level of illumination throughout an area. Another might be local or task lighting, which offers a high level of illumination over a small area with a surrounding zone of lower intensity; this could be a floor lamp beside a comfortable reading chair, or specific lighting for cooking or studying. Accent lighting, which calls attention to a particular object or feature such as a niche, shelves, or the interior of a skylight, is another possible layer. These accent lights add drama in the evening hours.

Lighting with lamps, or artificial lighting, as it is called, should be considered at an early stage in the design process so that it may be subtly integrated into the overall architecture. Use restraint on downlighting (overhead lights); indirect lighting provides more atmosphere than direct lighting, and this often requires integration. One solution is cove lighting. A cove is a pocket or cornice near the ceiling into which lighting is tucked. Tracks placed inside the cove can accommodate many different kinds of light—wall washers, accent lights, or a combination. Most often, people use coves to wash soft, indirect ambient light over walls or up onto ceilings. You're not aware of where the light is coming from; you just see glowing surfaces.

Lorcan O'Herlihy often uses cove lighting in his houses. In the Lexton MacCarthy residence, he also carved out recesses that he calls "voids" about eight inches into the ceiling, so that you see a lit rectangular niche rather than individual light fixtures. It's a sculptural solution, he says, where "you put the light up into the box, and the box gets lit as opposed to using just a single light."

Different light bulbs also create varying qualities of light and will directly affect colors of fabrics, wall finishes, upholstery, and other materials in your spaces. Learn about the differences between incandescent, halogen, low-voltage, and compact fluorescent bulbs. Lighting consultants can help in projects because they are familiar with the ever changing, ever growing selection of lamps and bulbs. Lighting is a technical field, and consultants can recommend the right lamps and their ideal placements. Some architects are better at this than others, so assess your architect's strengths and your needs to help decide whether a lighting designer is worth the added fee.

Light Experiences

Openings and the light that comes through them shape your experience of space. Imagine that you enter a room and are enveloped by light streaming down walls from above; in the next room, you look out through a large glass window to a view of a sunlit distant landscape. At a different time of day, you might notice the green of the grass through generous side windows in the first room and light spilling inside to warm the stone floor in the next room. Depending on where light falls at a particular time of day and where you are in relation to it, your experience of the spaces is different.

Specific light in rooms intensifies spatial experience. Charles Rose says he and his firm try "to find inventive and surprising ways to bring light in. Light finds its way in from above from monitors or skylights, and we may use it to highlight something special like a work of art or a moment of circulation like a great stairway."

Dark light, dim light, and colored light create mood. Think of the difference between a room dimly lit with candlelight and the same room with full sunshine streaming through windows. When I think of dark light, I think of Sainte-Chapelle, the thirteenth-century Gothic chapel in Paris. The light is not white; the impression is of an intense red and a deep sapphire blue. The effect is mesmerizing, completely unlike everyday experiences. I'm not suggesting you put elaborate stained-glass panels into your home, but the intensity and beauty of this experience is worth exploring. Light need not always be pure white like the light of the sun. Why not consider orange, violet, carmine, or cinnabar?

In the house Lorcan O'Herlihy designed for himself, openings have a balance of plate glass, Profilit glass (a self-supporting glazing system), yellow glass, blue glass, and green glass. The colors are created with a tinted film laminate on plate glass. "The color is wonderful in that house. On the front where the yellow glass is, when the sun pushes through it, it takes this whole yellow sliver of light into the kitchen," says O'Herlihy. "It literally hits the floor, then goes up a cabinet."

Mirrors introduce additional light into a room. They can behave like windows, reflecting sunlight, overhead light, and unexpected views into the depths of a room. Depending on the material, the effect can be subtle and sensual. Glass with a mirrored back and sandblasted front provides a muted glow, as does antique glass. In the dining room of one house, Peter Pennoyer put antique mirror on the ceiling. The mirror

111

reflects light from four pendants fitted with shades, which prevent glare. The lights hang from the intersections of four beams on the ceiling, and when they are dimly lit, a warm, beautiful glow suffuses the room.

Punctuations of Light

When you think of openings in a home, you might automatically think of punched openings set within a wall. The details, size, and placement set the tone. Punch, punch, punch: you can imagine a staccato rhythm. Walking by, you see frame after frame of what's outdoors, not unlike the frames of a movie. Elegant, long, spacious windows set symmetrically within a high-ceilinged room would give another impression, one that is stately and serene.

In Lorcan O'Herlihy's Lexton MacCarthy House, there are three large, framed views among other, smaller openings. One of these large openings looks out from the living room, one from the kitchen-dining area, and one from the master bedroom. The openings are nearly sixteen feet wide, and they infuse the spaces with light. "Wherever you are in the house, you are drawn to those openings," says O'Herlihy. Punctuation of light from above is another example, as in the architect's Jai House. O'Herlihy carved a rectangular aperture out of the ceiling plane over the pool "so you are not completely enclosed." As you're swimming, you can gaze up at the clouds and the changing sky above, and when it rains, the water drops right down into the pool.

Experiencing light from directly above is common if you live in New York or another large city. As you walk along the streets, you're enclosed from side to side; when you want to see something of the outdoors, you look up. City streets often resemble large interior courtyards.

On the interiors of houses, skylights, punctuations in ceilings, and ribbons of clerestory windows admit light from above. Besides wanting to see the starry sky at night or light grazing an entire wall, there are two reasons for having openings and light from above. First, you may want light in a space, but you don't need light and views directly at your side. In the hallway of the Jai House, a clerestory on the right lets light in from above, and glass set into the floor on the left lets light shine up. O'Herlihy used this placement instead of eye-level windows because there's a gallery of images displayed on the walls. "You don't need to see views as you are walking down that hall," he

Panes of blue and yellow glass add intensity, depth, and mood to architect Lorcan O'Herlihy's own home.

says. Second, openings and light from above allow privacy. This approach is especially appropriate in more intimate places such as dressing areas and baths.

When you walk from a room with solid walls and somewhat traditional windows into a space with glass from floor to ceiling, the experience can take your breath away. There are many ways of detailing this type of glass wall: the glass can be framed with metal or wood, it can have intermediate frames or mullions, or it can be frameless, held together with the most minimal of metal clips.

Sometimes a residence can be designed with this concept in mind. A house Lake/Flato Architects designed outside Santa Fe,

This wall of windows in a New York City townhouse designed by Steven Harris Architects floods the living room with light and also invites you into the garden courtyard beyond.

New Mexico, sits on what Ted Flato considers a challenging site with 360-degree views of open desert. The best views are straight west, where the sun shines from a low angle. The solution was a house where "you can go from porch to porch. You're always going to another place," says Flato.

Lighting Artwork

"In a residence, no matter what the value of the inhabitants' objects, whether paintings, craft, or decorative arts, it's not as valuable as the happiness present in a house," says architect Richard Gluckman. His firm, Gluckman Mayner Architects, has designed some of the most prestigious art galleries and museums in the country, so his opinions represent years of experience and serious thought on the subject. He believes that the people in the house are far more important than the artwork, no matter how distinguished or expensive the pieces might be. To light the walls rather than the spaces where people gather is to emphasize the wrong things. Gluckman prefers to light art "incidentally." Often he uses discreet, recessed down lights that subtly illumine artworks without diminishing the significance of the people living in the spaces he designs.

The opposite take on lighting artwork is to treat your home as a gallery, highlighting the works of art to give emphasis to rooms. If you choose this route, make sure to get the advice of a lighting consultant, even if only to help you choose the right fixtures and give you some guidelines for placement. Make sure that when all of your artwork is lit, the spaces are still comfortable places for conversation and gathering.

Night Lighting

The same room that feels open, light, and safe during the day can become frightening at night. With lights on inside, we feel exposed. People can see us, but we can't see them. One way to get around this is to design exterior lighting, so that we see what's around us even as night falls. Illuminate landscape features such as trees, paths, or terraces, and the stark difference between interior and exterior becomes less extreme. Another way to avoid this problem is to include shades or curtains as part of your interior design. Some choices, such as pocketed curtains or integrated shutters, require early planning, so think about them at the beginning of the project.

At night, there's an opportunity to play with moods and colors in lighting. A layer of red or blue lights in your living room might evoke the mood of a jazz club, while sparkling

115

fiber-optic lights might suggest an elegant soiree. Mostly, though, you will want low, soft lighting. Plan for dimmers on light switches, and keep a supply of candles at hand.

Another type of lighting that is most frequently used at night is, in fact, the oldest form of light, other than sunlight: firelight. It is little wonder that, over the years, "hearth" has become a synonym for home. Fire provides warmth, but that is only part of its enticement. The animation of a fire draws you toward it, and once you are near, it beautifully sculpts your face as its flames cast light and shadow across you. Fire has a life of its own, moving in unex-

pected ways. You can't control it, and that is part of its allure. Homes can be designed to tap into the profound pleasure that firelight offers. The fun of a campfire, for instance, can be reproduced in outdoor fireplaces built on terraces and patios.

The Courtyard House in Bellevue, Washington, by Olson Sundberg Kundig Allen Architects, is wrapped in glass walls that offer a view of the water immediately upon arrival and keep occupants connected to the spectacular site at all times.

This gas and glass fireplace in the Urban Courtyard House in Phoenix, Arizona, designed by Wendell Burdette Architects demonstrates how light and openings play on perceptions of space.

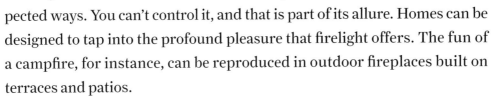

Indoor fireplaces can open to two different rooms, and they pop and sing as they take the edge off a cool spring morning or roar back at a winter storm. They may have raised hearths or may simply take shape on the floor of the room, whether they echo the proportions of the tall, shallow Rumford fireplace, which reflects heat effectively, or take a more dramatic form. Fireplace design is a science, and a short discussion with a fireplace consultant may be worthwhile to get the proportions right. Although modern heating has obviated the need for fireplaces for warmth, their sensuous, immediate nature will never be replaced. Wherever you have a fireplace, you can be sure of interesting conversation and reflection. If you sleep with smoldering, glowing embers in your bedroom, you invite deep slumber and animated dreams through the strength of their comfort.

House in Cabo San Lucas

Steven Harris Architects

In this house in Mexico, natural light

guides your movement from place to place.
For instance, a series of glass rods is embedded in the
east wall of the hallway that leads from the master
bedroom to the bathrooms and the exercise room.
If you get up at dawn and walk down that hall, you'll
see that the morning sun shining through the glass
rods casts circles of light on the opposite wall of the
corridor. The sequence of light contributes to
a sense of slowly awakening through the course of
the morning.

The room where the family has breakfast
faces south and is adjacent to the master bedroom.
The table is positioned at the west end of that space,
so there's no direct light or glare on the table in the
morning. As you sit and eat breakfast, you look out at
the ocean. There's a breeze, it's calm, and there's not
another house in sight.

The living room, which is situated at the end
of the other wing, faces east, so that when the
sun is setting you look toward Finisterra, or the
end of the Baja Peninsula. The room is designed
as a place where you can relax, have drinks, and
spend the evening. On the west wall, there's a thin
clerestory window, and at about half past six on
winter evenings, the setting sun comes through the
clerestory and turns one facet of the ceiling pink.
The room seems made for this precise moment.

120

House in Maine

Toshiko Mori Architect

This house engages its waterfront site in the Maine woods by creating a grand flow of space. Directly off one side entrance, a path leads out into the landscape. It loops through the surroundings before completing its journey at the other end of the house. You need only open the door and follow the gently sloped ramp to the nature path to take advantage of a clear connection between the building and its landscape.

Alternatively, you can saunter out to the south-facing, sunny, large deck, the size of which doubles the living space. Even inside, you are surrounded by trees and a panoramic view out to a protected ocean inlet, so transparent is the wall of windows that makes up the long side of the house. As Toshiko Mori explains, the layered walls and window penetrations "act like a series of screens, creating a transparency that allows the house to transition seamlessly into the landscape."

While connections to the outdoors are important for all, they are especially pertinent here because the client is an elderly woman sharing the property with her adult children and their families. The new construction is within sight of the older houses, yet they are distant enough that each maintains privacy. The landscape loop brings the generations of families closer to one another, while the deck and open living spaces call for social gatherings.

All the while, the house is comfortable too. The wall of windows allows for maximum heat gain—important in the cool Maine climate—and a ribbon of operable clerestory windows at the highest point inside allows hot air to escape. The house not only transitions into the landscape but creates a natural comfort from within.

128

HOUSE IN MAINE: TOSHIKO MORI ARCHITECT

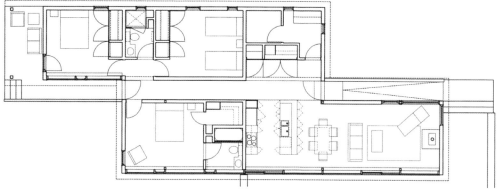

Spheres of Living

Design impacts lifestyle. Thin walls in a city apartment affect the way we interact with our neighbors, while a master bedroom close to the living space in a house can determine how much sleep we get. The comfort of a kitchen, where we spend much of our time together, influences family dynamics. Because of the way our space affects our lives, architects develop certain guidelines and ideas for thinking about activities in a home, some that are consistent from architect to architect and others that vary.

The specific stories that clients tell about the way they live, what they need to sleep, and how they entertain make a house come to life. The architect should be brought into a family's intricacies very quickly. When clients say that their partner snores or that they love being outdoors, they are providing crucial information for design. By listening to such details, and to the anecdotes families relate about themselves, their functions, their rituals, and even their quirks, an architect learns about the clients' lifestyle. From these clues, however small or idiosyncratic, an architect can begin to shape a house that is uniquely suited to the family, a house that is a home in the deepest sense.

From time immemorial, the hearth has been at the center of the main living spheres, as it is in this living room designed by Steven Harris Architects.

To begin thinking about how you live, look at the primary spheres of living in a home; these include spheres for entering and departing, gathering, entertaining, reading and playing, eating and cooking, working, sleeping and privacy, bathing, and outdoor living. You will think about space more creatively if you concentrate first on the primary spheres of living rather than on traditional divisions of space such as the living room, dining room, or bedroom. Designing based on spheres of living is not about simply moving rooms around on a plan but about forging a lifestyle from three dimensions of space. Because the spheres aren't concerned only with dimensions, structure, and conventions of a room, but also with function, activities, and daily rituals, designing around them gives us a broad palette of ideas to work with. Anything is possible.

Making the way you live a functional part of your home, then, begins by understanding the role you would like each sphere to play. Where will your family spend most of its time together? If it is the kitchen, you might want to include an informal eating area so you can cook and eat in the same space. And you might consider placing the main stair off the kitchen, making it the natural center of the house. Where will you watch television and films? Where will the children do their homework? If everyone will be together in the evenings, perhaps you'll include a large worktable and computer in one of the main living spaces. Within each sphere, think about conditions that create optimal living experiences. If you have children who will share a bathroom, would partitioning the bathing area from the washing area streamline morning bathroom routines? If you have a small family, could you place your washer and dryer in an upstairs hall closet to avoid lugging laundry to the basement?

Budgetary or structural concerns may make some lifestyle choices difficult to incorporate into your design. In looking closely at how you live within these spheres, you will develop an understanding of which need to be central to the design and which don't. Architects help clients figure out what they need in their houses first through conversations and then through design options. Architect Peter Pennoyer usually begins conversations by cataloging the traditional list of rooms; he finds this helps clients talk about the way they live. From there, room definitions broaden. When he says "living room," for instance, Pennoyer tells them what he envisions. "People react, and that's the best way to do it," he says. You need to know, facet by facet, how the clients live.

This is not to say that architects should ask people how they're used to living and then design for that! An architect's job is to help people think about how they

Layered spheres in the open space of this Dallas residence by Lake/Flato Architects allow for many activities to coexist. A hanging lamp and a hearth subtly define boundaries.

can use rooms and spaces differently. If there are pursuits you are passionate about, whether it's studying trees, playing backgammon with the kids at night, or having friends over on Sundays, an architect can suggest how these activities might be woven into the rooms. Consider traditions, events, and rituals as an opportunity for design; you can define your own priorities, your own program for living. Talking about the spaces you know facilitates talking about activities. It begins the conversation.

Spheres for Entering and Departing
Entering and departing a house doesn't begin and end at the front door: the landscape and the immediate interior spaces are part of the journey. Entry and departure are sequences in time. Built into them are stages of experience so subtle they seem almost invisible. Porches, paths, garages

(especially in relation to the front door): these are the transitions that prepare you for entry and departure. Your means of arrival also plays a part, whether it is on foot, by car, or on a bicycle.

Architect Peggy Deamer notes that the entry sequence to the Lieberberg House is calibrated both for visitors who approach by foot and for those who arrive by car. "You don't go directly from the street to the front door," she says. "You go from the street to an outdoor room, and then from the outdoor room into the house." In another house, Deamer describes a sense of being introduced to the landscape before being introduced to the house interior. As you enter the house, there's an unobstructed view of the out-doors. Even though there's a lot going on inside, you focus outward, then in again.

Gathering, Entertaining, and Playing Spheres
Before you talk with an architect about what you want in the main living sphere, think about how you want to use the space. Do you plan to entertain, and if so, how? Do you want the living room for reading or for the display of art? Is it a room you'll use all of the time? Do you want it

to be removed from other areas of the house? These days, few people want a very formal living room, but you may appreciate having one all the same.

Peter Pennoyer says that he likes to think about creating an area for children in the living room, so that the family can enjoy activities in that room that might otherwise be consigned to a playroom. There is no reason you can't have a room with an area for playing Scrabble, backgammon, and other games. In Pennoyer's firm, the architects observe the pastimes that a family enjoys and then integrate them into the design.

When thinking about a gathering in any room, you need to consider how you're really going to use the seating. Pennoyer says that many people overestimate how much seating they really need in the living space. He describes two kinds of gathering in a living space—one around a fireplace and the other around a view. In his Guaz House, he describes a semicircular window bay with a continuous banquette that subtly obviates the need for many moveable chairs. Thus, the living room requires only a furniture grouping that seats four or five people. Living spaces flow out onto porches, which are also furnished for seating. In another of his houses, Pennoyer describes an outdoor fireplace where people gather, which offers a different exposure to light and warmth than the hearth inside.

Spheres for Undefined Activities
If you'd prefer a separate room for playing musical instruments or games and watching television, there are ways to make the area central to the house rather than tucked away in a cavernous, dark room where no one enjoys spending time. Peggy Deamer and her firm achieved this in the Lieberberg House by locating the room between the family area and the guest wing. It acts as a "hinge" between the two zones and at the same time provides access to an outdoor garden area. The room is fairly well lit with an elaborate, louvered shade system. It can be darkened for watching television, but most of the time it's an airy space for drawing, talking, writing letters, and playing cards and other games.

All paths lead to this Westhampton, New York, room, making it a central gathering space in a home designed by Ike Kligerman Barkley Architects.

Playing can be solitary, as can creating. We may watch television alone, play electronic solitaire, compose songs on the guitar, or read alone, but a room that's comfortable can accommodate many activities, people, and even performances, if desired, at once. While one person is reading, another may be doing homework on

the computer as another family member plays a video game and yet another draws or paints. Who wouldn't want a room like this?

Dining Spheres The traditional dining room used every evening for family dinner has become almost obsolete. Without frequent gatherings of family and friends around the table, the dining room often becomes a throwaway space. With this in mind, Peter Pennoyer, in several of his projects, decided to make a library double as a dining room. In one of these rooms, a library table is positioned on one side of the space to hold stacks of books, additional volumes line the walls, and a table for two, three, or four stands next to the window. Comfortable club chairs near the fireplace allow family members to bring trays into the room and dine or have tea if they'd like. When the family does entertain, they either pull the library table away from the wall to offer seating for six or they connect both tables to create seating for twelve. While the clients do need to rearrange the room to entertain, they host such events only occasionally and make better use of the space at other times.

This type of room must be located fairly close to the kitchen in order for the dual purpose of library and dining area to be convenient. Pennoyer designed a house for a couple who plan to have children, so he knows that in five years the clients may want to rethink the room. Reworking the room does not require architectural changes, however; the couple would only need to replace the library table with a dining room table and eight chairs. The books can remain, and the room evolves.

It is possible to create an imaginative playscape even in the small backyard of a New York City townhouse, as Steven Harris Architects did.

This variable use of space is an example of not entirely giving up the idea of a dining room. By using the room this way, you can also take advantage of views, Pennoyer says. In the evening, you usually sit at a dining room table located in the center of a room; you don't appreciate the view because the table is somewhat removed from the windows, it's dark outside, and you're focused on the candles and the table setting. But you don't need to limit yourself to this sort of traditional arrangement. If you're designing a home oriented around a view, you can put a table right in a bay window. In fact, Pennoyer is currently designing a room on Fifth Avenue where a newly married couple will eat dinner looking out over Central Park.

Spheres for Cooking and Eating
Every client has a different opinion on the appropriate relationship between living, cooking, and dining spaces. In a house where people are cooks, the kitchen may be central to the living and dining spaces, not separated at all. "The crowd moves wherever people cook," says architect Ted Flato. Time is going to be spent in that space. "If the client wants separation between the kitchen and other areas, you still have to have a wonderful collecting space in the kitchen because people are going to be in there, regardless," he comments.

The design of a kitchen and its connections to other rooms relates to the scale of a house. With smaller projects, "You'd be foolish not to have the kitchen cleverly connected," says Flato. Rooms need to be versatile. In one of Lake/Flato's houses, the kitchen sits between the living room and the dining room with big, rolling barn doors on both sides. You roll the doors back and forth to connect or separate the spaces.

The Shrack House, another Lake/Flato project, is an example of a smaller home in which the kitchen is separate yet inventively connected to the whole. A staircase at the back of the kitchen ascends to a small second bedroom. "I love making the kitchen into the grand stair hall. I love dragging people through kitchens," Flato says.

Most people agree that you don't need a large kitchen to cook a great meal: most cooking tasks take place in a relatively small area. The sides of the "work triangle"—sink, stove, and refrigerator—in an effective kitchen should total between twelve and twenty-two feet. You don't want to walk too far between these important points, but you also don't want to be cramped. If you were to stand in the middle of a restaurant kitchen, you would be able to reach for a pan, open a drawer for a spatula, and even pull out a fish fillet without taking a step.

If you'd like a larger kitchen, baking and washing areas can be situated on one side of the room and cooking on the other. You can create a separate baking area, because often the people baking are different from those who are cooking. For baking, provide a marble countertop and a separate sink, and site the dishwasher nearby. You can work the cleaning area into this part of the kitchen as well. That way, people can clear the table and do the dishes without interfering with traffic flow in the cooking area. If you have the luxury of space, you can include club chairs, a fireplace, and perhaps a table. The room doesn't have to be huge, though. What's most important is that it functions well.

Working Spheres The ever greater influence of electronic equipment has affected home design. Because communication is now as clear and instantaneous across the world as it is within an office, a growing number of us work at home. This trend has created a need for home offices where everyone in the family, including kids doing homework, has access to a computer. The now common idea of a home office or library as a place to go online, do work, or take care of mail and bills has challenged the old idea of the library as a hushed room with paneling and leather-bound books where you go to read or reflect. Making the library/office a place that combines both is on the minds of architects like Peter Pennoyer, who asks his clients to think about including activities that they might not have originally considered appropriate to the room. For a family with kids, he gives a nod to the traditional library by designing two lecterns: one with a dictionary, the other with an encyclopedia. The rest of the space might be dedicated to computers where the children can learn and do research online. In this way, the room easily becomes a key part of the family's life.

The question of where to place a computer is more challenging if the option of an office/library is not available. Computers need not be tucked away; they can be located in a central place, near the hub of the house to allow families to spend time together.

Thoughtful contemplation and study are central to the concept for this tranquil scholar's library in the Catskill Mountains of New York State designed by Peter L. Gluck & Partners.

Often, kitchens and larger living spaces with dining tables become like small apartments within a house; most of the social activity occurs in this cozy spot. The main rooms can be wired, not only so you can order food online, look up recipes, and check movie listings but to allow children to sit at the table and do homework while being social with their parents. Architect Charles Rose says he believes all of these activities should be social, so he talks his clients into a large table, whether it is placed off the kitchen or in a dining room. If the library isn't going to be used much, though, Pennoyer suggests that it be left open to other rooms. It can be a circulation space, an entertaining space, and a sit-down-and-pay-the-bills space.

Spheres for Art and Collecting

We all own possessions we like so much that in our minds they are art. Collections of furniture, rocks, heirloom trinkets, documents, family photographs, and drawings by children are all works of art. These things, if you deem them beautiful and meaningful, shouldn't be relegated to the back of a closet; they should be displayed.

Think about your works of art in tandem with space. Allow the pieces to create ideas for you: the size of objects might suggest simple built-in niches; imagining a view of a grove of trees from a certain window can inspire a landscaping move in your yard. You're the curator, and this means you can show what you like. Pieces you relate to will hold together. Paintings, photographs, ancient porcelain and ceramics, large sculpture, drawings by family members, or wall hangings from foreign places shown as an ensemble will all enrich a home.

Steven Harris designed this intimate eat-in kitchen at Boxwood Farm in New Jersey to be glamorous as well as utilitarian.

If you own a major art collection and are designing your own home, you have an opportunity to design the residence around the art. Certain pieces inspire enclosures and ways of letting in light. Reportedly, the most impressive room in the house Philip Johnson designed for collector Dominique de Menil was the dining room, which was surprisingly small and intimate, and which featured paintings by the sixteenth-century artist Arcimboldo on all four walls. The works are profile portraits of spring, summer, winter, and fall comprised of the vegetation of each of those seasons. Architecture, in this case, embraces art by not overpowering it. The house may be about the art but can still be intimate and livable for the family.

Sleeping and Privacy Spheres

When designing sleeping areas, there are certain ground rules that everyone appreciates. If possible, the door into the bedroom should lead not directly from the hall but from a subhall. This little space then allows you to go into the bathroom or closet. The advantage of this arrangement is privacy. One person can go into the bathroom or to the closet without disturbing someone who is trying to sleep. If guest bedrooms or kids' rooms are all located off one hall, consider making the space more than just a hall. If it is widened at some point, the area could accommodate a small desk, bookcases, or a wall for art display.

The bedroom of a house in Connecticut by Toshiko Mori Architect is a private sanctuary for sleeping, waking, reflecting, and just daydreaming.

143

A house can function like a village or camp; people can come together or spend time apart. Peggy Deamer describes this sense of freedom in one of her firm's homes, the Lieberberg House, where an area off the main spaces houses the family room, two guest rooms, and a guest porch. The family and the guests each have privacy. "You don't just have your own room, but you have your own porch, you have your own area, your own wing," Deamer says. This layout is fairly consistent in her houses, even if, she admits, this image of living isn't for everyone.

Bathing Spheres Many people have the idea that bathrooms should be as large as possible, but it's not necessarily true. It's nice to have the luxury of space, but it's most important to have a beautiful room. If you want a large bathroom, "It should be more like a room that became a bathroom," says Peter Pennoyer. He renovated a historic house in Virginia where a previous architect had installed marble counters and a built-in Jacuzzi; it looked like the room had been taken over by appliances. Pennoyer's firm removed everything and put a freestanding tub in one corner and a shower stall with its own little marble roof in another, and included a separate table with a sink. This design honored the historic character of the room and looked like what it was—a large, vertical room turned into a bathroom.

This bathroom, designed for a residence in Austin, Texas, by Gluckman Mayner Architects, is serene and functional.

Storage Spheres

The way you store your belongings has a lot to do with how you live in your space. Storage can be completely concealed, partially concealed, or at the opposite spectrum, revealed and decorative. For instance, to conceal storage, you can build in cabinetry that's seamless with the wall surface. Carving out part of the cabinetry door allows you to open it easily; minimal hardware seems to disappear into the wall. Other closed storage options are armoires, dressers, and closets. Closet doors may hinge, pivot, or slide. You might even choose to cover the closet opening with curtains similar to those that dress your windows.

You can also store items in a way that displays them. An array of utilitarian gardening and farm objects can take on a sculptural quality on the wall of a barn. In a poché storage wall—a wall into which storage areas have been carved—the utility of the wall becomes its design. Architect Peggy Deamer suggests that such walls can even show off the changeability of the house over the course of a year with a seasonally changing display. The poché can include enclosed as well as open spaces.

Swimming Pools and Other Outdoor Spheres

Defining specific priorities for each outdoor sphere, whether porch, patio, terrace, or pool, interprets your ideas about landscape into a design for your yard. How closely will the sphere be tied to the house, how far away or separate, how wild in feeling? These are the big issues.

When placing a pool, for instance, you may want it close to the house so that you can see the kids from the kitchen. On the other hand, there's nothing worse than having a large, bright blue basin right next to your house that isn't in any way indigenous to the landscape. Particularly in the winter, when the pool is covered, you want it far from the house.

Peggy Deamer describes one of the outdoor pools she designed as more of a grotto, with one stone wall of the pool shared with the house. The larger landscape idea was that the pool area be kid friendly and both natural looking and visually pleasing. Originally, it was going to be built at some distance from the house. At the last moment, though, the clients changed their minds and decided they wanted the pool closer, so the kids would be near. The patio around the pool had to be comfortable but not overly sophisticated. Deamer had to select a pattern and quality of stone that would make the patio stable for lounge chairs and comfortable to walk on but would also appear natural; in addition,

146

The Jai House, designed by Lorcan O'Herlihy Architects, features glass doors that slide open to transform the living room into an exterior space and vice versa.

she didn't want a lot of grass and trees because she wanted to "de-suburbanize" the space. To solve this dilemma, she chose large stones and allowed grass to grow between them, achieving a simple paved area that didn't feel too manicured.

When you are working with outdoor spheres such as terraces, porches, and patios, you need to understand the different vocabularies. A wraparound porch, a trellis, or a terrace can be part of a house, looking out over a garden, or can provide a more casual connection to the landscape, with one space flowing into the next. Practical landscape elements such as stairs take on additional meanings in outdoor spaces. While residential stairs typically don't require a lot of space to ascend and descend, the stairs Steven Ehrlich designed for the Canyon House are grand, extending twelve feet across. With that dimension, the stairway encourages people to sit and functions like amphitheater seating. In his Webster House, Ehrlich installed a platform raised fourteen inches off the ground, at bench height. Not only can people sit on mats, cushions, or chairs on the platform, but for a larger gathering, guests can sit on its edge. The platform seats twenty people, and when there's no party, it fades away as a quiet architectural element.

Comfort and Instinct

Sometimes, the idea for a space doesn't arise from a direct and immediate need but instead finds its function at a future time. You might look at the exterior of your house and think it needs balance, something on the other side. It might be a breakfast nook, a porch, or a master bedroom suite. Architects design from the outside while at the same time thinking about the inside. When you and your architect develop a program that makes sense with the form, you've hit on the idea. Architect Peggy Deamer explains that when her studio designed a residence with an indoor-outdoor space that allows exterior access to the kitchen, dining area, and living room, the extended facade needed some visual relief. The team designed a small space, a niche made of glass, which gave the family something they hadn't predicted. This space became a favorite sunbathing spot for the family's numerous dogs. The niche became a kind of pet den off the kitchen, the room where the family tended to gather. It was designed to complement the aesthetics of the exterior, but the area ended up providing something important for the interior. Says Deamer, "I am always struck by the fact that the most marvelous spaces, moments, and events are the ones that are the most idiosyncratic, where clients were just willing to take a leap of faith."

Keeping an open mind when assessing your instincts, whether for a new type of living space or in a detailed consideration of spheres of living, will contribute to a sense of ease in your home. Comfort comes, I believe, from not being overly formal about how you live. If you can set aside traditional or accepted notions of what rooms mean and put your house together in your own way, you will feel at home there. If you love to cook, and want to have your guests nearby so you can prepare meals and socialize at the same time, you would probably not choose a traditional kitchen. Or if you'd like a traditional cooking area, you might create one that's large enough to entertain in; even that changes the notion of a kitchen from that of a workspace to a more inviting, comfortable space.

Opening the kitchen to the living or dining area allows people to share cooking, chopping, and washing responsibilities or at least to converse while one person prepares the meal. Often, this strategy works well when the relationship between the areas is open but at the same time each area is distinct. Through the arrangement of furniture or the relationships of spaces, take care to establish a definite sense of place for each area. When you are sitting in the living space, you want a feeling that you're relaxing, and when you're eating, you need to be able to focus on the company around you.

To tailor your space to your family, you need to be realistic about the way you really live. Imagine that you are already living in your home—think about what you'd be doing there this evening and how you'd entertain this weekend. Spheres are not about how you would *like* to live; they're a vision that you can actually *achieve*.

Comfort in the most literal sense means placing a priority on human dimensions and ergonomics. No matter how nice the design of a sofa, if it's not comfortable to sit on then it's not worth having in your home. If you are constantly going to worry about someone spilling red wine on a piece of furniture, then slipcover it or choose a color that won't show stains. Make sure that your things are in order and within reach. If you know you think more clearly and sleep more soundly when your papers, clothing, and other possessions are organized, design storage systems for yourself. Take care of your needs.

The comfortable second-story sitting porch of a residence designed by Turner Brooks Architect has a view of the surrounding neighborhood and its community activities.

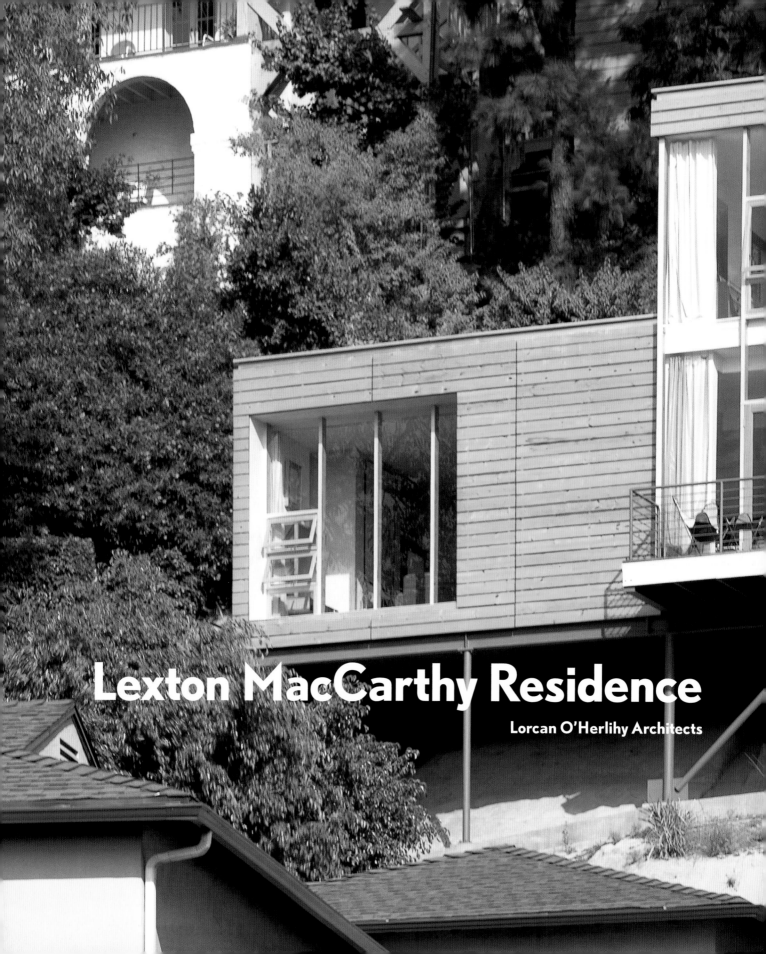

Lexton MacCarthy Residence

Lorcan O'Herlihy Architects

To witness the contrast of the Lexton
MacCarthy Residence in Silverlake, California,
during the day and at night is to begin to understand
the subtleties of light as a material. Situated on a
steep lot in the Hollywood Hills, the house has a
nearly panoramic view of the city of Los Angeles
below. A two-story glass curtain wall, living-room
balcony, and large punctuated opening allow
spectacular vistas during most daily activities:
dining, cooking, relaxing, and even sleeping. Both
upstairs and downstairs, these openings infuse
the spaces with light that, in effect, orchestrates
the movement in the house. "Wherever you are in
the house, you are drawn to those openings," says
O'Herlihy.

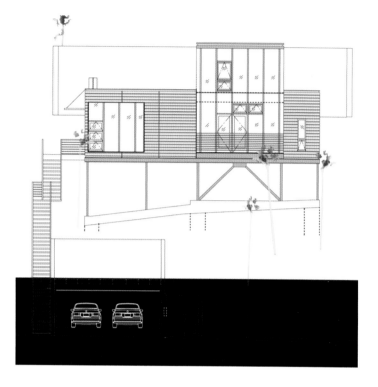

    Regulating the amount of intense sunlight
is given equal thought. O'Herlihy hung two ranks
of curtains on the nearly sixteen-foot-wide walls of
glass. In front, curtains reflect ultraviolet light with
a silvery background material; in back, fabric panels
double the amount of sun protection. In the living
area, the architect places the glass plane farther into
the interior space for two reasons: it allows for more
shade than if it were pulled to the exterior, and it
gives differentiation to the facade, appearing darker
as a material from the outside.

    Other innovative materials and techniques—
such as the large translucent sliding screen that
opens or closes a room to other spaces, the thick wall
made up of sections of structural glass that encloses
the master bathroom upstairs, or the exterior siding
made of one-by-six-inch pine slats with half-inch
gaps that become shading and filtering devices when
they continue past a window—allow the house to
come alive with various uses and with the changing
light of day.

152

LEXTON MACCARTHY RESIDENCE: LORCAN O'HERLIHY ARCHITECTS

LEXTON MacCARTHY RESIDENCE: LORCAN O'HERLIHY ARCHITECTS

It is not enough to see architecture; you must experience it . . . you must dwell in the rooms, feel how they close about you, observe how you are naturally led from one to the other.
Steen Eiler Rasmussen

I don't think of the spaces I make as empty. Rather they are full, stretched, or otherwise shaped. I like to think of them as existing as currents, whirlpools, waves: entities that are compressing or expanding, and that are flowing up, down, around, causing drafts and eddies.
Turner Brooks

Flow of Space

Embracing you, surrounding you, lifting you for a view, turning you around a corner, or drawing you toward a fireplace: houses can be engaging if they are designed that way. From bedroom to bathroom to closet to kitchen, we start each day on a circuitous journey that will, by the end of the evening, lead us back to our starting point. Along the way, some rooms and passages will encourage us to interact with others, some will keep us connected to activities elsewhere, and some will allow us to get completely away. These experiences play a significant role in our lives, determining how we relate to other members of our household and to our surroundings every day.

Flow of space is about how we move and what we see. Spaces can be embedded with signals that cue us to move one way and not another. Natural light in a foyer, for example, can pull a person toward it, while the materials or dimensions of a doorway subtly inform us whether it leads to public or private space. These visual and spatial cues and physical paths help guide us through our activities, creating a daily promenade that is, by turns, public and private, expansive and intimate, directed and reflective.

In a house in northern California by Fernau & Hartman, the same material is used for the ceiling plane and built-in furniture, creating a sense that the space folds and wraps from ceiling to wall.

The idea of sequence is important to flow of space because it refers to the experience of a home and also to a related idea: the experience of movement through a home. A house guides you moment by moment, something you may never have noticed. Orientation, circulation, privacy, and the flow of spaces have a tremendous impact on family life.

Choreographing Movement Consider a house with just the skeleton in place. If only the wall framing and floors were finished, it would remain structurally sound, though uncomfortable to live in. There would be no clear order to activities, no sense of privacy, no structure to our movements. As we partition and screen the space, we are determining how the different functions of our lives will blend.

Now imagine the house you plan to build with the skeleton transformed into a fully realized structure. With partitions added, the space is now a positive presence rather than an absence. You'll begin to feel individual spatial volumes, sense the openness or enclosure of rooms, and become aware of the way one area connects to the next. The space is where the materials aren't. As you imagine moving around and spending time in different rooms, you'll notice constructed relationships between rooms as well as between the interior and exterior, and you'll find places that make you feel centered, secure, active, or calm. You'll feel the house move you at a lively clip or slow you to an easy, rambling pace. Perhaps there is a narrow hallway ushering you quietly into the library, or an abrupt turn on a staircase that signals the beginning of the private quarters. The house guides you while at the same time letting you choose how to inhabit it.

Assembling the spheres of living into dynamic maps of how we live is the most basic function of flow. New York architect Steven Harris describes this idea at work in the entry sequence to his Cabo San Lucas House. "As you're coming down the ramp and into the place, it very, very slowly and gently unfolds the view," he says. "As you park the car, you get a distant view of the horizon. Once you've started down the steps, you don't see the ocean any longer. It's a soft delaying of that view." At the same time that the house and landscape appear effortless and inevitable, they provide a spatial and visual map of sorts, with cues and options. The house invites you down a path and up stairs built into the rocks, giving you a sense of where it may lead.

Not every home will offer the opportunity for the kind of dramatic journey through interrelated, sculptural spaces that Harris describes, but even the simplest homes can have an alluring unfolding of space. A few ideas are central to understanding how to manipulate and shape flow to fit your needs.

Loops, Axes, and Speed

Turner Brooks considers each of his houses a "flexible container of space, bending, swerving, expanding, and contracting willfully in response to the desires of the program and character of the site." He adds, "Space rarely stops." As it turns corners, changes levels, or opens up, it is, like nature, running its own course. The best architects channel or sculpt space, connecting the spheres through equal parts art and science. One basic concept in the spatial map of a house is a *loop*. Loops allows you to come and go in two directions—you're never at a dead end. When entertaining, this type of circulation helps to avoid bottlenecks, says architect Peter Pennoyer. "Sometimes it's a matter of just having a discreet door at the end of a living room, where you can slip out and wedge your way back through a bar or back to the library, " he says.

The layout of Lake/Flato's Creekside House in Houston allows the inhabitants to move freely from one sphere to the next. Although the residence is quite open, defined areas suggest gathering, eating, and other family activities.

Built around two destinations, an *axis* leads from point to point, offering a clear, linear sequence of movement and sight. Called the "regulator of architecture" by renowned Swiss-French architect Le Corbusier, the axis creates the simplest possible sequence for movement. Axes and sightlines play a very important role whether you choose to obey the formal conventions or discard them by experimenting with symmetry, balance, and other rhythms. A visual axis, or line of sight, may draw you in a particular direction at the same time that a physical axis, or pathway, stops you, perhaps at a glass wall.

"Slow space" tends to have furniture, while "fast spaces" are paths for movement. This is *speed* as it relates to architecture, a third basic concept for controlling space. Slowing an area down so that it encourages gathering, a comfortable place to sit, or speeding it up with rhythms of materials that hasten you forward affect your movement through the house. If you understand the nuances of axes and loops, the pacing of movement through them, and the orchestration of physical paths and lines of sight, you can create surprises in your circulation, like the discreet living room door Pennoyer mentions.

Although the openings separating them are spacious, rooms in this home in Massachusetts, designed by Peter Pennoyer Architects, are distinct spaces with individual ceiling treatments and defined geometries.

Designing around flow requires first a sense of the way you live. When we live in a house where the organization works, life happens more smoothly. Everything seems easier. Basing design strategies on your living patterns and individual priorities will make your home both a reflection of your lifestyle and an active participant in it.

A remote living room may see little everyday use, but when linked to a den, it can serve more naturally as a reading room or a quiet place for a nap. Likewise, kitchens without active relationships to dining or family areas leave the cook isolated when it's time to prepare meals. Connecting the two spaces with an island, for instance, keeps the cook involved. Sequencing space helps us feel responsive to our surroundings, allowing flow to become the catalyst it should be.

Between essential spheres in a home are the central living paths. A single passageway may serve a variety of purposes. It might let you rush to work or carry a child to bed—though its first task is relating the activities of one room to the next. Walking in the front door, dropping keys on the hall table, cooking dinner, sitting down at the table, unwinding on the sofa is a sequence we repeat many days of the week. Morning rituals of passing from private quarters to public areas are likewise repeated again and again. These familiar paths are the lifeblood of the home, and while it seems simple to make sure that rooms are used (put the rooms there and people will go into them), it doesn't just happen. You have to design them for use.

Prioritizing Your Space

In large homes, and even in medium-size ones, it's possible that some spaces will not be used, particularly if they're not designed properly. You can be sure that a large room with a kitchen at one end and a bedroom wing off the other will be used because you have to walk through it every day. A nonessential room on the periphery of a house, however, can be left out of everyday activities. There's no sense in creating rooms you won't ever use—the extra space would be better left as part of your yard. Circulation and movement through a house engage the spaces. Having to get from one place in the house to another—needing to use a stairway to go upstairs, having to go into a kitchen to cook, or passing through a doorway to get outdoors—determines whether you frequent the places on the way.

Steven Harris often uses the analogy of a shoelace when talking about circulation: as you move from one space to another, your path strings together a sequence of rooms or separate buildings. The architect thinks of circulation as a series of episodes, with each one (preparing for the day, returning from the office, throwing a dinner party) adding up to a well-thought-out script of activities. "All the parts," he says, "come together to tell the whole story." To design around each episode, then, you need to think about the activities and rituals that take place in your household every day.

Peter Pennoyer designed an enfilade, or linear arrangement, of separate living spaces in this island house in Maine. The rooms are layered by identical shaped openings; a window of the same proportions stands at the end of the sequence.

The entry sphere in this residence designed by Ike Kligerman Barkley in Upper Brookville, New York, is the point where paths begin and converge, lending liveliness to everyday routines.

Carefully orchestrated space fosters intimacy with both our immediate surroundings and with family. Brief encounters on a comfortable stairway landing reinforce family bonds; a wall of windows along a hallway encourages us to enjoy the view of children playing; openness between kitchen and family room or eating area allows us to catch up with one another as dinner is prepared. These moments come about through thoughtful design, and they can be greatly enhanced when we acknowledge flow as the choreographer of our lives.

Essential Sequences The rooms and sequences most central to your lifestyle, the essential sequences, should be determined by the individual needs of your family. California architect Lorcan O'Herlihy recalls that early in the design of one house, his clients expressed a strong desire to spend time outdoors in the West Coast climate. This was a fundamental piece of information, and O'Herlihy was able to use it to design a house where the family could move freely between indoors and out. When you enter the house, you walk directly into an outdoor room—a breezeway with a lap pool—and then you go indoors. Similarly, you must walk outside, under covered passageways, to get from the master bedroom to the living room. A sheltered path through nature links these two major spheres. Large sliding doors provide a barely perceptible barrier between interior and exterior.

This way of living might not be right for you, but it is an example of how lifestyle choices can help organize your public and private areas. Essential sequences, arranged around regular activities and rituals, will differ from home to home based on how you prioritize each important sphere. A terrace–family room–kitchen sequence in one home, for example, may become a family room–terrace–kitchen sequence in another because one family favors a more detached, private terrace and the other prefers to open up the cooking and entertaining spheres to each other.

As you think through your essential sequences, draw them in bubble diagrams. This type of diagram will help you map out and visualize larger relationships. Without addressing specific volumes or layouts, a bubble drawing will help keep priorities clear and allow you to present an architect with the associations and activities you envision. Focus first on the high-priority sequences that will inform design the most. Whether it is an expansive kitchen for a gourmet, a combined living room/dining room to maximize a waterfront view, or an elaborate home office suite, the sequences most important to you will orchestrate your daily life, so make sure that the way you live informs them.

Invitation to Family Life
When you enter a house (or any building), you need to grasp the basic organization of the space almost immediately. This is crucial to the design. It makes you comfortable and centered. Above all, you must have a clear entry sequence for guests. (You can't have a guest arrive at your home and not have any idea how to get in!) Once inside, there should be visual cues that indicate which areas you can enter and which are more private. Guests don't necessarily need to be able to find bedrooms easily, but they do need to be able to navigate toward other spaces, such as the living room. Traditional houses take you from the front entrance into a main stair hall. Public rooms are on the ground floor, while private quarters are usually upstairs. There's no reason a house has to follow this particular layout, but every home does need an understandable organization. For family life as well as entertaining, you might choose to separate formal from informal areas, public from private areas, and service from living areas. Each house has its own hierarchy of order.

The entry realm can be an organizing principle for family life as well as an invitation inside the home. Witness a summer residence at the New Jersey shore. Joel Barkley of Ike Kligerman Barkley Architects designed a dramatic triple-height entryway where the entrance itself plays only a secondary role. Hallways wrap around, stairs connect to hallways, and comings and goings of family members are always in view. Whether the clients are entertaining or just spending time in the house, the entryway is not only an invitation to the home but also an anchor. Detailed wood surfaces, the only wood in the structure, create a warm core. In contrast to the other rooms of the house, which provide inhabitants with places for eating, sitting, reading, and talking—the stable routines of life—the entry is in perpetual motion. There's the Venetian bridge connecting the children's hall to the parents' area. There are the places to hang out or collect thoughts, hide, playfully spy on others, and perform. It's a space that is highly theatrical and yet is the heart of the home.

166

For clients who love to spend time outdoors, this easily accessible screened porch on Fire Island, designed by Peter Pennoyer Architects, is large enough for a table and many chairs.

Public and Private Realms

In a home, there should be a natural progression of intimacy. This means that there's appropriate separation between the public places—where guests visit and all family members congregate—and areas where you need peace and privacy. The separation can be immediate, such as a doorway, but often a layering of space makes sense. As you progress deeper and deeper into a home, you become more comfortable. The front yard leads to the front porch, which leads to the front door, then the foyer and entry hall, then farther inside. A master bedroom suite might have a small hallway of its own, separated by a few steps from the rest of the bedrooms. This type of hallway has many benefits, complete privacy being one of the most important. Whether you live in the city or in the country, the progression is important. A bedroom would be awkwardly placed next to a kitchen.

It is not uncommon that the sequence from the front to the back of the house is also a sequence from public to private. In this case, the private rooms may have a particularly close relationship to the landscape behind the home. Such a sequence draws family members into the ever changing events of the seasons outside: lush spring greenery, bright summer flowers, falling autumn leaves, quiet winter snowfalls.

Links and Thresholds
Spheres of living are coupled by thresholds—doorways and partial enclosures—or links—passageways, staircases, and entry realms—that should create, area by area, generous and exciting pathways for our lives. Thresholds and links carry us from one activity or ritual to the next, and if those transitions are not well orchestrated, our homes can lack the clear paths that guide us. A threshold can be an arch, a rectangular doorway, or a partial wall that distinguishes between adjoining spaces; links are extended passages like stairways, hallways, and entry realms that join one sphere to the next. Either can be narrow, wide, just taller than we are, or full height, though the larger the opening, the more generous the flow.

Transitional experiences are often signaled by specific design strategies, but there is always one overarching concern: the relationship between one sphere and the next. Changes in surface materials—stone to wood, rough to smooth, warm to cool, reflective to translucent to opaque—make us aware that we have made a transition. Using a border material between two similar surfaces or changing the direction or pattern of the same material will also serve this purpose.

The entry realm of this New York apartment by Peter Pennoyer offers an invitation into the life of the family and the common area at its center.

Variations in level also indicate a connection. Full staircases create the most obvious changes, though two or three steps down from a dining room to a living room can be the only transition needed. Consider the natural contours of your site. On hillside properties, for example, gradual shifts in level can help a house merge with the landscape.

A third element for marking a transition is lighting. A living room lit by windows at the sides offers a significant change from an entryway with an opening to the sky above. Similarly, variations in artificial lighting—for instance, spaces with overhead chandeliers next to spaces dominated by floor lamps—create a strong transition.

Finally, dimension may be used to indicate a transition. In general, the greater the width and the shorter the length of transitional space, the more inviting the flow. Wider links and thresholds make us feel less cramped; short ones keep us moving from room to room.

Thresholds and links are critical devices for moving us through a home. Subtle or strong, they are responsible for rhythm. They can also help further an illusion. For example, in Steven Harris's Cabo San Lucas House, the distinction between interior and exterior has been all but erased. The colors used inside and those that appear outside are almost the same; the stabilized earth of the courtyard and the polished concrete of the floors are similar. The main difference between interior and exterior is that, when you are inside the house, a roof covers you from above. Similarly, in a Long Island residence, Peggy Deamer designed a large glass screen between the dining room and the living space. Moving from one side of the partition to the other creates the illusion that you're passing into a separate sphere; however, in either area you're really part of the same larger space.

Interior Spatial Cues

Interconnected spaces that serve a variety of functions are becoming more common. Gathering, eating, entertaining, and all types of public activities often take place in what may really be just one structural room. To root these lifestyle choices in familiar surroundings, we use framing strategies that help distinguish between the different regions. Even as we enjoy the openness of a generous flow, we look for familiar signals that let us know how to take part in the functions of individual spaces.

Partial enclosures, another type of threshold, can orient us in this way. Half walls, railings, and other types of partial enclosures allow us to connect to the activities in nearby spheres without feeling completely exposed to them. These enclosures can be as simple as a service island between a kitchen and dining area or as elaborate as a sandblasted glass scrim separating a den and living room. Each creates a different level of access between the overlapping spheres.

Other spatial cues can pull you toward the center of a space or push you toward the

The stone exterior of this residence in Montauk, New York, by Deamer + Phillips Architecture presents a private facade to visitors. The interior, however, is completely open to the backyard and ocean beyond.

periphery. In Steven Harris's house in Cabo San Lucas, ceiling heights are intentionally very low. On that site and in the region, the horizon is omnipresent. There's water all around. The ceilings force the view to the horizontal landscape outside. The space works to throw your view to the perimeter.

The opposite approach is exemplified by a room with a very high ceiling—a dome, for instance, or a cathedral ceiling. The tendency in such situations is to bring the focus of the room to the center. In another residence designed by Harris, Boxwood Farm in New Jersey, the ceilings are relatively high and the spaces are more internalized. There's much more attention paid to an internal world than in the house at Cabo San Lucas; the structure is much more enclosed, has many fewer windows, and is more protected from the elements.

How Spaces Flow Together
You must make basic organizational decisions when designing around flows of space. You need to determine which spheres will be distinct spaces linked through formal transitions and which will flow easily from one zone to another, perhaps with partial enclosures. Architect Richard Gluckman recalls that one client said to him, fairly early in the process, "I want corners, period. I have to have corners in my rooms." That desire established the basic parameters for space in the project.

The potential approaches to organizing your space vary tremendously; it is important to keep different types of movement in mind when you determine how spaces come together. The best way to make sure the spaces link successfully is by varying sizes, dimensions, and shapes from room to room. Space should be sculpted into flowing sequences, not homogenous rooms. Follow a tall entryway with a low-ceilinged den, an intimate living room with an expansive deck.

Peter Pennoyer prefers to define separate rooms in the houses he designs. Rather than take all the square footage and make one big space, he delimits rooms so there is a feeling of more space, more luxury, and more comfort. Consequently, the spaces themselves and the relationships between them become crucial. You can have rooms that are very open to one another, but they must possess a character that is distinctive enough so that the house doesn't become a running string of rooms. Pennoyer believes he can give a client an octagonal dining room, a living room with ceilings thirty inches higher than adjacent rooms, a double-height stair hall, and a study with low ceilings—all in the same home. That these spaces might be open to one another doesn't diminish each room's individual character.

A fluid, varied spatial experience is also central to the work of architect Charles Rose. Instead of designing a series of geometric spaces, he allows the geometry to grow out of the site and what he calls the "making of space." He and his firm tend to make space that is proportionally tall, typically with ceiling heights that are greater than the side-to-side dimensions. The office also favors a constant diversity—that is, if you were

In this house in Orleans, Massachusetts, Charles Rose Architects has designed distinct spheres that commingle and overlap. They are separated by subtle spatial cues such as changes in floor level, translucent walls, and variations in the ceiling plane.

to slice into the buildings at random intervals, the dimensions of each space would be different at every cut.

A translucent partition in a house in Sagaponack, New York, by Deamer + Phillips is a screen between living areas that simultaneously connects and separates the spaces.

A change in temperature can also heighten spatial diversity and enhance transitions. Rose's firm doesn't install heating and cooling systems that keep every room at seventy-two degrees. "We like it that when you move into a room, maybe it's warmer, maybe it's cooler, maybe it's taller, maybe it's shorter," he says. The house might take you through a compressed space, then into a very open space; the light might vary and a material may change accordingly. There's an intentional, sequenced variety throughout, which is essential to creating surprise and drama in your daily journey.

Matchbox House

Gluckman Mayner Architects

"Landscaping is an extension of the architecture of the building," says Richard Gluckman. At first glance, you might not understand how this principle relates to the Matchbox House, the home he designed for himself and his family on the North Fork of Long Island, because the rectangular volume is elevated above the ground. But his statement is absolutely true.

Gluckman raised the house because the site is a flood plane and no living spaces can be placed at ground level. So what looks like a house separated from the earth is actually a sensibly and sensitively designed structure. A restriction became an opportunity. The main rooms of the house capture more cooling winds and look out to more spectacular views than they would have if they were placed on the ground level. Spaces open to porches and decks so that you are never far from the outdoors.

A stepped terrace on the upper level of the house provides a complete connection with nature. There, architecture *is* landscape. Gluckman likens the experience of this terrace to work by the artist James Turrell. When you're on the terrace, there is one horizon: that of the building itself. As you climb the steps, your eyes leave the artificial horizon for the true horizon. The entire landscape is revealed. Says the architect, "I never get tired of that moment. The two horizons are slightly displaced. It's a wonderful unanticipated effect."

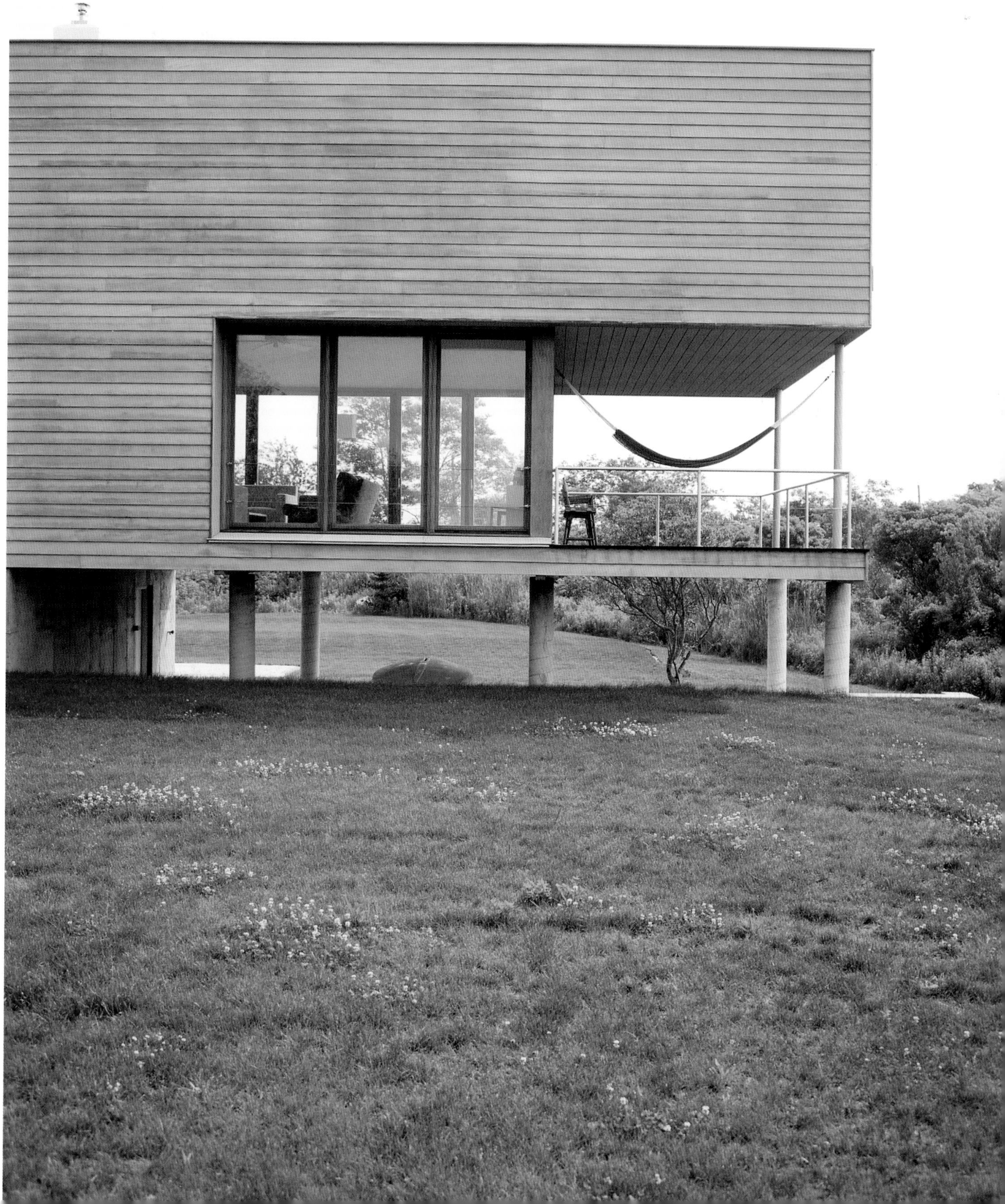

MATCHBOX HOUSE: GLUCKMAN MAYNER ARCHITECTS

Semaphore House

Turner Brooks Architect

When you approach this house in Dummerston, Vermont, says architect Turner Brooks, "The overwhelming first impression is the gesture of the semaphore arm swooping up out of the meadow, signaling its presence across the enormous grassy expanse of the gently rolling site." Although the Semaphore House is not a traditional structure, the sculptural form is nonetheless closely tied to its location through regional materials and detailing. You might see the same wood siding, standing-seam metal roof, and roof overhang details on older farmhouses in the surrounding New England countryside.

Inside, too, the forms are sculptural. Gestures, lines, heights, and light and dark areas provide spatial cues; you sense instinctively what Brooks terms the "possibilities" of the house. From the open entry space, you can proceed east to the light-filled zone of the living room, which expands under the rising roof of the semaphore arm; you can ascend a metal stair to a cozy window seat looking out toward Mount Monadnock; or you can walk a short distance to the dining area and kitchen. A narrower, more private corridor leads north and south to a one-story volume with bedrooms and studio.

The exterior composition suggests various spheres of activity: the swooping, ascending roof of the semaphore arm speaks of household goings-on, light, and views from inside; opposite, the human-scaled porch is a welcoming shelter; an angled wall projects out to conjure a private moment. The two intersecting elements of the semaphore arm and the single-story shaft, one lying close to the meadow, the other rising to the sky and mountainscape, play with one another continuously. "Perhaps it is best seen in the June dusk," Brooks says, "when fireflies, seemingly in response, are frantically signaling all around it."

Sustainability

Homes that take into account sustainable technologies provide healthy, comfortable environments for living. Imagine a house capable of generating cross breezes with the windows open, or a house with glass engineered to allow lower winter sun into rooms while shielding the high, hot summer sun. Imagine heating, cooling, and ventilation systems that make moisture content, outdoor breezes, and temperature central to the design. These are sustainable concerns.

Sustainability refers to a manner of building that takes into consideration the region and the environment—its climate, natural resources, and construction traditions. The term describes buildings that are healthy places to spend time because materials that emit poisons have been avoided and provisions for air quality have been built in. And it connotes comfort through an understanding of natural ways to cool and heat spaces.

The natural materials on the exterior of this Kinderhook, New York, residence by Steven Harris Architects weather with the elements. The unmanicured alfalfa grass landscape presents a golden meadow at some times of year and a field of wildflowers at other times.

If the term seems multifaceted, it is because the root word "sustain," which architecture has coopted, is itself multifaceted. It means to maintain something that exists, to supply it with nourishment; and it means to support the spirit, vitality, or resolution of, to encourage.

Unfortunately, as Virginia-based architect William McDonough has observed, the term "sustainability" has come to mean "managing the bad stuff" rather than "celebrating the good stuff." He prefers the verb "sustaining" because it connotes action. "And then," he says, "if we are going to talk about sustaining, we can talk about 'What does it mean to build a home? What does it mean to be alive?'"

Architects and specialists in the field have many practical suggestions about how to incorporate sustainable principles into everyday living. What they can yield ranges from birdsong and breezes to the peace of mind that comes from trusting that your home will not undermine your health. The good news is that sustainable ideas are not confined, as some believe, to a certain style or look; they can be integrated into any design, and when desired, they can even invent a new language. By making sustainability part of your original concept, you can create a living environment that enhances the quality and duration of life of your house.

The Unique Nature of Place

"I experienced beautiful dimensions in a courtyard on Mykonos, having lunch with an extended family . . . The filtered green light from the vines made people look so well. Outside, the wind was blowing, but inside the courtyard it was perfectly serene. White walls, stone floor, a long table, a dozen chairs. The simplicity was remarkable." These are recollections of Greece by Australian architect Glenn Murcutt.

Ted Flato of Lake/Flato in San Antonio, Texas, also acknowledges the impact of nature on the idiosyncrasies of a specific site: "One of the keys to design in Texas is dealing with the hot sun. It's a hot place and the sun is one of the first things that you start with—certainly the one we start with. It has to do with orientation, with aiming the building in the right direction if you have a choice."

Recognizing the particular nature of your region is critical, regardless of the budget for the building and regardless of whether the structure is a single-family home, townhouse, apartment building, or other structure in the community. "One of the challenges with the mass marketing of houses and the standardization of housing is the sense that housing is independent of place," says Gail Vittori of the Center for Maximum Potential Building Systems in Austin, Texas. "People connect to

Shim-Sutcliffe Architects designed a floating garden and swimming pool beyond to animate the Weathering Steel House in North York, Ontario, with reflected light, motion, and sound.

an image they like. They like it aesthetically or they may like some of its performance functions, but it may not have anything to do with where they are." She says you can see this disconnect play out in the landscape: in the way a building is oriented and in the materials that are used.

Therefore the first principle of sustainability is to understand the idea of connecting to place. How do you learn about place? Look around you. Observe the locale with fresh eyes, particularly if it's an area you've known for years. Be realistic about what kind of landscape you have before you. If it's a prairie, think how you should choose to live on a prairie, just as you would look at the humidity and foliage of a jungle for a different set of clues. Who might you consult about building sustainable strategies into your new home? One place to start is the architecture department of a nearby college or university where young architects are being taught to incorporate "green" ideas into their projects. The local planning department is another resource, or there may be a green building department in town.

194

Recognizing What You Have We are linked with the fundamental laws of living things, and we have responsibilities. In the best cases, we don't have to give anything up to fulfill them. We can take advantage of what we have and use it in a responsible way, says Vittori, by building with local materials or existing materials, by learning ways to block or channel the sun and summer breezes, by making provisions for storing and using rainwater in drought-stricken areas, or by placing the thermal mass on the inside of the home to radiate its warmth in cold areas. These are just some of the methods that connect a home to its place. Chances are older, indigenous houses will show you how the inhabitants of the region have addressed some of these same ideas. As you begin to learn more about sustainability, you will want to find architects, interior designers, engineers, and contractors who are familiar with these concepts or who will work with a consultant.

"Responsibility to nature is not difficult or something to avoid," says William McDonough. "It should make us feel good about ourselves. For instance, a person living in Manhattan can feel good about not using a car often, being surrounded by three to four different people in an apartment, and having one to two exposures to the outside, which means you're sharing your thermal flux with your neighbors. You have a

A massive chimney made from salvaged stone rises through all three floors of this Nova Scotia house by Gluckman Mayner Architects. The indigenous material ties the home to its region and its specific site upon rocky cliffs.

very small ecological footprint." He continues, "If you're living in a house in New Jersey or Long Island, you could look out one morning and say, 'Where is the sun? What's my house doing thermally?' I can open the windows in this weather and turn off the air conditioning. I could have a thermometer; I could have a barometer; I could figure out the relative humidity and I could decide when I have a red day and when I have a green day. And then, how much energy do I need? If I put in solar collectors, I could cover that load. I could invest in a windmill in Iowa and help farmers with a new cash crop. Now I can go to work guilt-free and I've got an investment that's earning me money." Sustainable houses, then, are about living well just by changing the way you see the world.

"Climate-responsive design doesn't have a style; it has a performance requirement," says Paul Stoller of Atelier Ten, a New York firm that emphasizes a sustainable approach to design. A sustainable home has no one "look" to it. You don't have to bury your home underground (though you can) and have a sod roof so that the earth provides stable climate control, although there are beautiful houses nestled in hills that work this

Materials and spatial configurations are among the forces driving sustainable design, as in this Southampton, New York, home by Peter Pennoyer Architects.

Deciduous trees and an overhanging roof shade this lakefront house in Texas designed by Lake/Flato Architects; a large screened porch captures cool breezes from the lake.

way. High-performance design can lead to a new vocabulary, and there are stunning examples of this methodology, such as photovoltaics installed on the skin of the building. An energy-efficient house can also look regional in its language, but again, it's not necessary. Atelier Ten says that there are plenty of good examples to learn from and borrow from. The studio refers to this give and take as "hybridizing." When you make a hybrid of an existing regional house with fresh ideas using current technologies or streamlined detailing, you get traditional elements recast in new ways. Thinking about sustainable concerns is neither a constraint on creativity nor a return to the past. It's a stimulus toward an architecture that is innovative and relevant.

Sustaining Comfort

We create buildings to make ourselves comfortable. Some days are the perfect temperature and humidity, and we'd be as happy outdoors as in, but no place is like that every day. We need materials around us, we want to be able to control our environment, and in a well-designed sustainable house, the structure itself should do most of the work to make us comfortable. Until a hundred years ago, the architecture had to do *all* the work, with no help from modern mechanical systems. A fireplace helped in heating, open windows allowed fresh air in, and roof overhangs and appropriate materials provided natural cooling. It is not necessary to return to that era. We should have the best of both worlds: timeless strategies developed over centuries for each climate as well as the most up-to-date materials and mechanical systems. Today we have high-performance materials and numerous systems available for heating and cooling. Your home should be naturally comfortable most of the time without systems, though. Try to rely on them only during climatic extremes.

There are numerous techniques for creating comfort with the architecture itself. These principles are known as "passive design." Atelier Ten emphasizes building tightly and with high insulation levels as the most important elements for reducing energy use, improving comfort, and controlling moisture in houses throughout the United States. When you build tightly, you have no air or moisture infiltration. Anything beyond that is an added benefit.

A skillfully conceived residence should be able to self-heat in the wintertime by retaining the heat from people, lights, televisions, and solar gain, and recirculating it either passively or via heat-recovery systems. In the summertime, the house should be able to self-cool by use of intelligent shading devices, either trees in the landscape or awnings, high-performance glass that blocks sunlight, or screening elements. You remove the solar gain when you don't need it and admit the gain when you do. The basic principles are to make use of free energy and reduce the need for supplemental heating and cooling. The size and placement of windows, the configuration of space, use of water, and many other elements play parts in passive design. It is important to know that good design takes these fundamental ideas into account.

If you've ever had an argument with your spouse, children, or roommate about whether the windows should be open or closed and the air on or off, you know exactly what I mean when I say that what's comfortable for one person isn't always comfortable for someone else. People wear different levels of clothing, they're doing different activities, or they like to be warmer or colder. Comfort is an individual matter.

This predicament doesn't have to be a problem. A well-designed house allows for different kinds of comfort in different areas, rather than a uniform setting, says Atelier Ten. If you have an exercise room, you can provide a different comfort condition there than you have in the living room or bedroom; various spaces will rely on different heating and cooling techniques depending on the uses of the room. Regulating temperatures for different spaces in your house need not be more difficult than opening a door or window for a breeze or closing a curtain to seal off cold drafts.

Air Quality
Central air and heat are nice, but the most critical aspects of comfort in your home have to do with air quality, which includes humidity levels, surface temperatures, and air temperature. Humidity greatly affects your comfort level. If you are in a climate like Miami's and the temperature is eighty-five degrees outdoors with high humidity, you're going to be sticky and feel terrible even if there's a breeze. When it's humid, you perspire and the water stays on your body—the air is too saturated with moisture to allow evaporation. However, if you're in a place like Santa Fe, where it's dry, eighty-five degrees feels comfortable because your body can get rid of heat through evaporation. On a cold day in a typical New York building, the air is very dry and uncomfortable because of the radiators. A heating system that factors humidity into the equation would make all the difference.

A sliding louvered panel offers shade to a residence and studio in Tucson, Arizona, by Ibarra Rosano Design Architects. Moving the panel to one side provides an unobstructed opening to the outdoors.

A room walled with uninsulated glass will be uncomfortable if the weather is very hot or cold, no matter what else you do. However, the same room with properly insulated glass, operable windows, or two masonry walls for collecting and radiating the sun's heat could be quite comfortable. Surfaces and materials make a huge difference. A floor with radiant heat makes for more comfort in the winter because you are guaranteeing a warm surface. Even if the air temperature is fluctuating, you can still count on that stable, warm floor.

Healthy Materials and Finishes
Besides contributing to comfort, air quality is a litmus test of a healthy environment. Gail Vittori says, "We know how much time people spend indoors, and we know that indoor air is usually worse than outdoor air, in fact, and people don't realize that." She contends that a lot of the blame goes to the materials we bring into our homes, materials that emit volatile organic compounds, and cites the epidemic rates of asthma. "Something is going wrong," Vittori says, pointing to the introduction of large amounts of synthetic products—paint, flooring, ceiling tile, wood paneling—into the places we work, go to school, shop, and so on. "We have a bad situation. How do we make it better?" she asks. "We try to identify what the safer materials are. That's one way."

At some point, perhaps, all building materials and finishes, as well as cleaning products and air fresheners, will be healthy for us. They're not right now, so do your homework. People are inventing new, healthy materials all the time. Look for materials that are described as hypoallergenic; these tend not to have irritating chemicals in them. Materials with low VOC (volatile organic compound) levels also further this goal. VOCs are emitted as gases that make some people very sick. Formaldehyde-based resins are another problem, so seek out different kinds of adhesives. Choose materials that can be easily cleaned without chemical solvents. Atelier Ten advises that a VOC-free floor that requires intensive chemical cleaning can, in a single scrubbing, emit as many VOCs as the material would over its lifetime. Choosing a material that can be cleaned with soap and water, a citrus-based cleaner, or another natural product eliminates the need for chemical pollutants in the future. Also, refer to the rating system developed by the Greenguard

Sustainably harvested woods, low-VOC materials, stone, passive solar strategies, and a radiant in-floor heating system operating on geothermal energy contribute to a comfortable, healthy environment in this Charlotte, North Carolina, house by William McDonough + Partners.

Environmental Institute, which gives the chemical emissions for different materials. There is still too little information about the hazards of the chemicals around us. Even a simple shower curtain may emit extremely volatile chemicals.

Your home can make you sick in other ways. A very small roof leak in a hidden corner can allow mildew to take hold, which might cause residents to suffer from aches, cramps, or fevers. This may be an extreme situation, but the point is that you need to make sure your home is a healthy place to live. Moisture control to prevent mold and mildew growth is essential. You have to design the building envelope and the building control systems to keep moisture out of the house or to vent it when it's already inside. If you end up with moisture infiltration through a leak or through a bad wall design that allows condensation to form in the wall, you'll have mold and mildew growth. There is almost no way to get rid of it once it's there. For some people, this is just an annoyance, but for others, the spores that are released are life threatening. You need to pay special attention to potential moisture problems in bathrooms and kitchens. Wherever you have moisture, you want to make sure to get it out.

Refreshing Your House
You will want to make sure you have fresh air in your house. The higher the carbon dioxide levels, the less fresh the air is and the more sluggish you will feel. Your house needs to "breathe." Traditionally, house construction wasn't very tight, so houses breathed whether you wanted them to or not. This kept carbon dioxide levels low but was abysmal for energy conservation. When a house breathes, it exhales whatever is inside and takes in whatever is outside, so in the winter your home loses valuable warmth and in the summer it gains unwanted heat. Now that houses are typically built quite tightly, they don't breathe. As Paul Stoller of Atelier Ten says, if you don't design a breathing mechanism for the house, there's a danger that the carbon dioxide levels will build up and you'll be walking around in a carbon dioxide "stew," which may not be life threatening but is certainly not healthy.

As a low-tech solution, opening your windows works well for fresh air. However, if you plan to rely on it exclusively, you need to ask yourself if it's feasible, says Stoller. Will you reliably open the windows? There can't be noise or pollution issues right outside. For instance, if you're living on an urban corner above a bus stop, you will be inviting toxic exhaust into your house if you open the window. You also have

Gracefully rooted in the vernacular of the larger landscape, this house in Hillsdale, New York, by Deborah Berke & Partners translates a traditional building language into a modern one.

to consider the weather: in winter, people usually keep windows closed to cut down on cold air and drafts. If you're relying only on open windows to ventilate the house, then you have a problem unless you live in a climate like California's or Hawaii's.

The other way of getting fresh air is with mechanical ventilation, which ensures that background ventilation is always on. A fan moves air in and out of the ductwork. It draws in an air change, or half an air change, or whatever you set it to. This can be worked into your central air system or can exist as a small, dedicated ventilation system. Atelier Ten normally specifies these small systems for the entire house. They will supply air to bedrooms, living rooms, and major spaces and exhaust it in kitchens, bathrooms, and any other areas of potential high moisture and odors. Heat recovery may be added to the ventilation systems as well, so that you don't lose the heat or cooling that you're storing in the house. Stoller says that the systems provide a modern, reliable solution suitable for any project.

Cycling and Recycling

Living by sustainable principles doesn't have to change your lifestyle dramatically. It just requires a slight shift in mindset. Healthier materials and environmentally friendly products are already more available to us because we're choosing them. We're asking questions. If you think about the entire life cycle when purchasing goods and resources that you use in your everyday life, you're already making a difference.

Everything has to go somewhere. As each of us becomes more aware of this principle and as manufacturers, builders, developers, and city planners make the necessary changes in accordance with this awareness, we move toward a healthier, more sustainable way of life. Things will no longer be out of sight and out of mind, and we will no longer have to feel bad about turning the heat up in our homes or going shopping. "If everything is nutrition, then you can celebrate it," says William McDonough. He's not recommending that you be a reckless consumer, just that if you want to purchase something new—a colorful carpet, a comfortable sofa— you should be able to do it without guilt. Under many current scenarios, where older objects or possessions have to be thrown out, you do feel guilty. You've taken a resource and rendered it invalid, and then you've taken more from the system for your new acquisition.

Consumption in that sense is a destructive act, but it doesn't have to be. McDonough says if you were to buy a carpet made from the wool of "happy sheep" in New Zealand and designed with biodegradable backing, and you made sure that your old carpet went into the compost heap, then you've just "cycled nutrition." In that case, he adds, New Zealand may have lost a little sulfur and some soil health, but you are conscious and engaged. He takes this line of thinking a step further and adds that if you were to transport and recycle the rug using solar-powered energy, then all you did was create jobs. That's a "celebration of abundance."

Anticipating the Future
When you design well-proportioned, light-filled spaces, they can be adaptable and useful far into the future. McDonough provides the example of former urban industrial buildings and warehouses that have been reincarnated as loft spaces. He says that they have good bones: high ceilings and tall windows that bring daylight deep into the spaces. They are nicely proportioned and illuminated, with good air circulation. McDonough says that you can't perform an opera in there, but you can do just about anything else. Aside from converting such a building into the familiar loft apartments, you can make it into a school, an art gallery, an artist's studio, or even a dance floor. In short, they are buildings infinitely useable for human purposes.

Similarly, a room that is pleasingly dimensioned can be used for numerous purposes, whether as a bedroom, office, dining room, or play room. In this way, the same house can be appropriate for many kinds of families at various stages of life. Just as old industrial buildings are adaptable, whole houses can be adaptable, too. For instance, a townhouse can become a two-family house, a doctor's office, an art studio, and even a one-family townhouse again as urban cycles occur, tenants age, and different spaces are needed. Houses can also have apartments over the garage so a college student can have an affordable place to live or an older resident can stay in the neighborhood when the upkeep of a house becomes difficult and unnecessary. The right kind of flexible spaces provide you with the means of creating a richer community within your neighborhood.

You can prepare for generational changes in your home simply by designing a house that can adjust to your changing needs. For instance, a room downstairs may easily

205

become your bedroom when climbing stairs becomes difficult. You may choose a site near the center of your community, not an enclave-pocket on the periphery. The siting encourages you to walk into town.

Lake/Flato's Idaho house offers gentle transitions between expansive exterior, sheltered porch, and intimate interior.

An appealing living environment is one that you feel comfortable with now and can foresee evolving along with your needs through the years ahead. You can view such a flexible home as a great investment from a financial point of view because it will be worth more in time. Or you can see it as an investment in your health and happiness, which is, after all, what the best homes provide.

A house that supports the generational changes of your life is perhaps the most literal example of a home that can sustain you. But sustainability touches upon every aspect of building your home. By understanding a region, its traditions, and its climate, you nurture the environment, and you learn how to site your house to capture sunshine or ward off the cold. By using materials that are safe, you learn how to protect your health. By thinking about the shaded and exposed areas of your design, you learn how to adjust the spheres of living so that rooms provide different levels of comfort. By orienting openings thoughtfully, you learn to articulate your home's interaction with nature and light. Sustainable architecture even touches on the most elusive and personal contributions you make to your home, the subtle impressions and ideas that inspired its design, because it fosters a sensitivity to your surroundings that results in unexpected delights. To design a sustainable house is to be open to the idea that the house might show you how to live, as McDonough would say, being "timelessly mindful, where we actually get to celebrate every thing, every breeze, every birdsong."

It is my hope that you will live lightly on the earth in a home that sustains you, your family, and your dreams and never lets you take for granted the wonder of the world around you.

Villa on the
New Jersey Seashore

Ike Kligerman Barkley Architects

"Architecture is like weaving. You're always trying to communicate between different consultants and craftsmen to pull together something that has never been made before," says Joel Barkley of Ike Kligerman Barkley Architects. By weaving, he means designing and building with many different architectural languages at once.

The invention of an architectural language through quoting and combining other influences is clear in the firm's house at the New Jersey shore. Built in a town where there is a lot of Mediterranean architecture, the designers looked to that architectural language but also to the work of the British architect John Nash. Nash built numerous country houses in England at a scale similar to what the clients and architects had in mind.

On the exterior of the house, you find gray slate, which is typically a northern material, and stucco facing and limestone trim, typically southern materials. Juxtaposed, the combination is rich. Certain parts of the house are literal quotes from the work of Nash, such as the tower form with the elliptical window. Yet the house is in no way a copy. Playing and expanding upon the English character of Nash's work, the architects added Gothic tracery in the entry hall, dining room, and sitting room. You might have the illusion of being in an English manor, walking along Venetian bridges, passing by an Italian grotto, or strolling through courtyards in southern Spain.

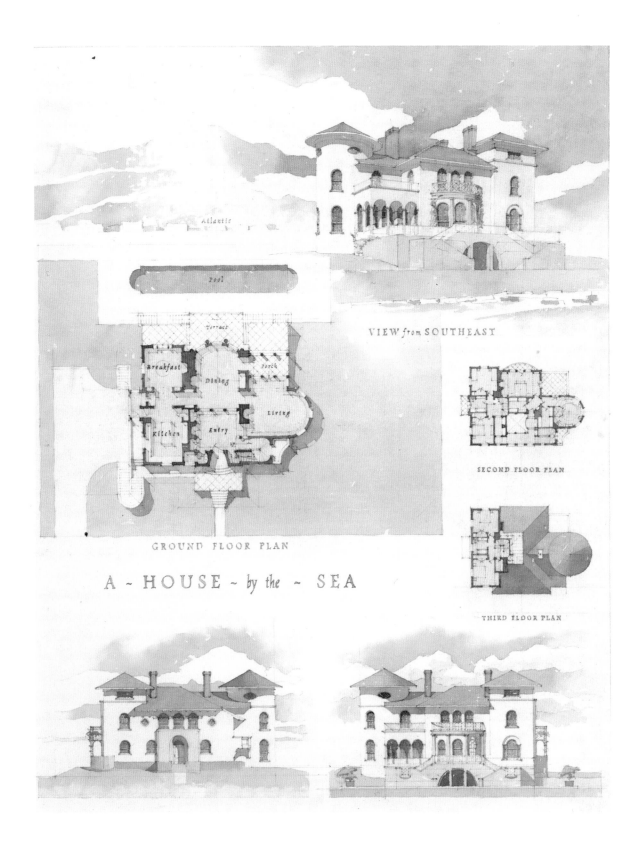

Atlantic

Pool

Terrace

Breakfast

Dining

Porch

Living

Kitchen

Entry

VIEW *from* SOUTHEAST

SECOND FLOOR PLAN

THIRD FLOOR PLAN

GROUND FLOOR PLAN

A ~ HOUSE ~ *by the* ~ SEA

VILLA ON THE NEW JERSEY SEASHORE: IKE KLIGERMAN BARKLEY ARCHITECTS

Afterword

The making of a house should be an enjoyable and exciting adventure. It is an opportunity to create a place that makes you happy every time you wake up or return from a long trip; a place that celebrates the environment; a place that is cozy and enclosed in the cold months and open and transparent in the pleasant months; a place that not only fits into the landscape but enhances it; a place that encourages interaction but also allows for private contemplation; a place that reflects your interests and idiosyncrasies. A place that you are proud of.

The adventure begins in the planning stage. Pulling together a team of like-minded design professionals allows you to relax and not worry that you don't have all the answers. You are only obligated to express what you are truly confident about, to talk about your dreams and experiences, and to reflect upon past places and spaces that you have enjoyed. It is a collaborative process: you throw out pieces and parts, the design professionals pull the pieces together, and the ideas begin evolving into your house. It is a journey: you don't always end up where you first imagined, but you should end up in a place that will make you happy.

Good, thoughtful houses usually outlast their owners. They are part of your legacy and contribution to society. The energy and effort that go into making these kinds of places will benefit and give joy to another generation. It is this longevity that shows us how important it is to go beyond large closets and spacious bathrooms; to look at the big picture, the relationship with the neighborhood and the street and the landscape; to build with materials that last; to work with the climate; and to create houses and communities that will make the next generation proud.

The process of building a new house or fixing up an existing one is a grand undertaking, and this book is a great place to begin the journey.

Ted Flato
Lake/Flato Architects

The living room of the Bluffview House in Texas by Lake/Flato Architects has two focal points: the fireplace inside and the view outside.

Anyone can design. Anyone can be taught
to investigate and discover. It doesn't take great
flair. Good design is more a matter of the ability
to understand the issues—of pursuing the question
until you make an appropriate discovery—and
there are always many appropriate answers. If you
understand how things are made and put together,
you can at least produce good quality.
—*Glenn Murcutt*

Resources
As the elements of design begin to weave together, inspirations will build and design priorities will slowly come into focus. You will also want to review practical items as you put the elements to work in your home.

It is important to understand how the design and construction process unfolds. You'll want to consider the selection of the architect, the budget and total fees involved, and the contractor you'll hire. Setting expectations for the time required for design and construction and familiarizing yourself with specific aspects of the process, such as review of shop drawings and incorporation of sustainable principles, will also prepare you to transform the vision of your home into reality. One of the very first things you'll want to think about is how to describe the kind of architecture you're imagining in words.

Architectural space has a tremendous influence on how we feel. But it takes words, the right words, to communicate how you want to feel to an architect. Various descriptions may suggest moods you would like to inspire in your home: serene, intimate, sculptural, open, tailored, cozy, classic, dramatic, mysterious, stunning, free, strong, heavy, light, rich, active, quiet, flowing, contained, secure. With these words as tools, your architect will begin to use another set of words: space, form, scale, volume, proportion, rhythm, cadence, balance, symmetry, asymmetry, light, color, texture, surface, detail, skin, structure, joint. It is important to familiarize yourself with these terms to get the most out of communication with the architect.

THE STAGES OF DESIGN Architecture offices divide the design and construction of a building into stages. As a client, it's important that you understand these stages. Not only do they describe the design process, but they usually drive the overall collaboration. Meetings between the architect and the client typically coincide with each stage, and fee structures are based loosely upon them as well. Generally, one phase does not begin until the previous phase is approved by the client and the architect.

The intent of *concept design/schematic design* is to give you an overall sense of direction for the design and enough of a floor plan to be able to judge, roughly, the size and relationship of major spaces and functions. In *design development,* the design is worked out in greater detail to fix and describe the size and character of the project in regard to materials and systems. The relationship to the site becomes more clear.

The stage of *construction documents* is devoted to preparing drawings and specifications to set forth, in detail, requirements for construction of the project. During *bidding and negotiation,* the architect assists the client in the selection of a qualified general contractor and works with both to secure complete prices for construction of the project. It is the client, rather than the architect, who has a formal agreement with the contractor.

In the stage of *construction administration*, architects check shop drawings, samples, and other submissions by the contractor; visit the site at intervals to review the progress of the work; interpret the construction documents as required; review contractor's applications for payment; prepare final punch lists; and verify completion of the project.

BUDGET AND FEES Settling on a budget is a vital step in the early stages of deciding to build a home. Your architect will benefit from knowing your target figures as she begins to design; this way, the concept of the house will more easily align with the reality of the budget. As part of schematic design, she will provide a preliminary estimate to ensure you are on the right track; this rough estimate will be refined and finalized throughout the stages of design. You may want to privately budget a buffer in the range of 5 to 10 percent when deciding on your overall budget in case the home design project goes over the target cost for one reason or another.

Architects employ various fee structures, though it is most common for an architect to base design fees on a percentage of the overall construction costs. Generally, architects charge between 10 and 25 percent of the total construction budget, depending on the level of completion and detail of the drawings and, often, the quality of the design. Those fees will normally include: all stages of design; drawings and other documents required for standard residential building permits; immediate hard landscape design (walkways, terraces, etc.); interior architectural finishes, such as millwork and fixed cabinetwork, finished painting, selection of standard nondecorative light fixtures, and floor finishes; basic furniture placement for existing movable furniture; structural, mechanical, electrical, and plumbing engineering services provided by consultants.

Additional services that architects usually bill separately include: public reviews and approvals beyond standard permit applications; interior design services in connection with new furniture, furnishings and accessories, window treatments, special wall coverings, rugs and carpets, specialty painting, including surface preparation, and decorative lighting; lighting, kitchen, acoustical, and other design or engineering consultants; surveys, soil testing, and verification or documentation of existing conditions. Typical reimbursable expenses include: travel, printing and photocopying, photographic services and reproductions, telephone calls, model supplies, and postage.

It's not uncommon for an architect to be paid on an hourly basis, especially when the project is a renovation of an existing building. When demolition begins on an existing structure, there are a fair number of surprises and unknowns. Often, many more drawings are required, which necessitates a more flexible payment structure.

CONSTRUCTION PROCESS Just like the process of design, the construction of a residence is divided into a number of phases, many of which overlap. Generally, these are: site work; foundation with concrete or masonry substructure; framing, that is, the structural system, whether of wood, steel, or another material such as load-bearing masonry or stone; sheathing, or the covering (wood boards, plywood, or wallboards) over exterior studs or rafters, which provides a base for the wall or roof cladding; roofing; mechanical systems, including heating, air conditioning, fresh air, humidifiers, and dehumidifiers; electrical; plumbing; insulation; exterior finishes and detailing, including placement of exterior covering; interior finishes and detailing.

Clients should prepare for what New York architect Larry Wente refers to as the "muddy middle" stage of construction. This is the period when construction is well underway—when the frame, roof, and sheathing may be up—but it seems like nothing more is happening. Actually, a lot is happening, including installation of mechanical systems, electrical wiring, plumbing, and insulation, all of which are behind the walls as part of the infrastructure. Wente suggests that clients ask their architects to let them know when the house is approaching this stage and then let them know when they're halfway through it, three-quarters of the way through, and so on.

CONTRACTORS You can select your contractor through competitive bidding and negotiation or simply through the recommendation of your architect or a friend. A strong working relationship between contractor and architect is as crucial to the process as a strong client/architect relationship, though, so if your architect recommends a builder he or she likes to work with, this can often be the best route. The inverse, however, is not necessarily true. A very good contractor can recommend an architect whose design aesthetics and approach are not compatible with your own.

It is important to note that separate relationships with your architect and contractor can lead to a messy triangle. In most successful building projects, the architect acts as intermediary between the client and contractor. When you trust your architect and allow him or her to oversee the contractor, the process will flow more smoothly. The architect and contractor can begin working together early in the design stages to forge a collaborative, noncompetitive relationship.

Once the architect has developed a set of construction documents, contractors will bid for the job, unless you've already chosen a contractor through a referral. Understandably, contractors want to win the bid, so they may be optimistic about pricing and bid low. These bids are only binding inasmuch as they follow the letter of the construction drawings.

Once you've agreed on the fees, a detailed contract is essential. Typically, projects are organized so that there's one contract between the architect and owner and another between the contractor and owner, but none between the architect and the contractor. It's important to understand everything about a contract before beginning a project. Don't be afraid to ask about any points that are unclear. Hire a lawyer if you can; if not, compare your contracts to the American Institute of Architects (AIA) documents available at www.aia.org, which are generally considered fair.

The contractor's contract should address the topic of "change orders." These are the design changes or supplementary costs that occur in every project: if something additional is inserted into the building or if there's an unforeseen circumstance, like engineering reports that necessitate more structural work. The contractor will need to charge for these occasions; in fact, change orders are a normal part of a contractor's fee structure. Yet some contractors take advantage of change orders, bidding low with the knowledge that they will charge additional fees if the architect's drawings aren't fully coordinated.

In reality, an architect cannot possibly account for and call out every minute detail, especially with a tight budget or schedule. Good contractors know this and understand that they'll get more referrals from architects than clients. So bear in mind that if your architect recommends a contractor she has worked with in the past, it is likely that they have a positive working relationship. In the best cases, everyone works well together. The construction documents act as a basis for communication between architects and contractors—the more complete the drawings and the more time the two have to meet and discuss construction, the less confusion there will be during the building process.

DESIGN/BUILD In design/build firms, the architect also acts as the general contractor. This is a simple way to avoid conflicts. There's a single point of responsibility for design, construction, cost, and schedule, and there's full-time on-site representation by the architect. For smaller projects, this can be a big benefit. Still, the design/build structure also has risks. The architect and contractor don't learn from each other's expertise, and the creative tension between the two, which often leads to new ideas and innovative solutions, doesn't exist.

If you're evaluating a design/build relationship, make sure to speak with your architect's references: Were final construction costs in line with the original bid? What was the breakdown between design and construction? Did the client feel that the architect's construction duties impaired the design, or vice versa? If you're building in an area without a lot of professionals qualified to build the type of structure you want, design/build may be a good option. But do your homework. And if your project is a large one, don't be afraid to ask for a project manager responsible for coordinating the logistical issues associated with building.

RENOVATING If you're deciding between building and renovating, you've probably discovered that it can cost just as much to renovate an existing structure as it does to build a new one. Demolishing and reframing a portion of a beautiful eighteenth-century farmhouse, for example, may require engineering and design work that adds considerable time and cost to the project. Even with professional advice, it's difficult to know what's lurking behind the walls or under the layers of paint. Older structures can rot or begin to fail structurally, and in addition to matching the original millwork you fell in love with, you may find yourself reinforcing the existing structure, moving walls to make room for heating, ventilation, and air conditioning systems, replacing windows to bolster insulation, and on and on.

Still, renovation is the only way to preserve antique details and handwork, so many clients are more than willing to take these extra steps. If you've decided to go this route, be sure to find an appropriate architect, one familiar with the type of home you're renovating. In addition, invest in quality engineering studies. Make sure you know what sort of work your roof, foundation, mechanical systems, and basic structure—often the biggest costs in a renovation—will need. You may fall in love with antique wooden floors and room proportions, but if the structure isn't sound, a renovation will become more costly. Be honest with yourself.

Always update with care. Present-day amenities—high-tech cooktops, bathroom spas—can be added to almost any space, yet their insertion is not always appropriate. Finally, pay attention to scale and proportion. Although you may love the idea of opening up rooms to one another, let the original organization and details guide you. Tearing down walls is one solution, but it is usually not the only solution.

SHOP DRAWINGS A shop drawing is a drawing that a mill worker, metal worker, or any custom craftsperson makes to communicate to the architect exactly how he plans to finish the work. It ensures that the piece will come out as intended. Architects' construction drawings establish a framework of design, relationships, proportion, and details. The shop drawing shows how all of the invisible joints work. Often, the design will necessitate something that's not readily available, such as a specific steel angle size, for instance. Then the architect and fabricator have to come up with another idea. The design process can be similar to a game of telephone. Someone says something to one person, who then whispers it to another person. When the message returns, it may be garbled and different. Shop drawings allow you to get the idea straight.

TIME FRAMES Architects note that the time it takes for design and construction is almost always much longer than most clients imagine. Why can't it be done faster? "Everything has a gestation period," architect Steven Ehrlich explains. "Just like it takes nine months to have a baby, it takes a certain length of time to design. If you rush it, you are just being foolish." Ehrlich advises his clients to expect the design phase, including developing construction documents and obtaining building permits, to take approximately a year for a house (that is, if it's a simple process). The construction phase will take anywhere from one to two years, depending on the complexity and size of the house. For very large, complex projects in which everything is custom designed, it's not uncommon for design and construction to take three to four years (or longer). Another architect explains, "If you try to speed up the first stage of design, you really get into trouble down the road."

Design is a creative process. You can't equate designing a house with, say, purchasing a piece of furniture, car, or appliance. The beautiful design that comes out fluidly and quickly is the exception, not the rule. Ask your architect for a frank estimate of the time frame. Even in the early stages of design, she can approximate how long design and construction will take. Just bear in mind that the design may or may not have been set, the documents will not have been bid, and the budget will most likely be a ballpark figure. It is not until the construction documents are prepared that the contractor will be able to put together a detailed construction schedule. These schedules are generally quite accurate, and any delays in construction are typically due to weather conditions, unforeseen complications that require added drawings or changes to the design, or design changes discussed between clients and the architect.

Such design changes can be the biggest contributor to construction delays or cost overruns. While changes are a natural part of the design process, it's important to understand that seemingly small alterations, such as adding pocket doors or opting for steel rather than wood windows, can add weeks or months to a project. Any change will require additional research and adjustments to technical drawings and schedules. The elements of good design are all interconnected. One change necessitates another and another until all components work together once again.

SUSTAINABLE DESIGN REFERENCES Sustainable building addresses environmental and conservation concerns to enhance the quality of life in your new home. Recognizing the particular characteristics and construction traditions of your region, incorporating energy-efficient "green" materials and technologies, creating comfort and wellbeing through design: these are the goals of sustainable architecture. In addition to your architect and contractor, numerous on-line sources offer information on building sustainable ideas into your house.

Active Living by Design: *www.activelivingbydesign.org* Promotes innovative approaches to increase physical activity through community design, public policy, and communications strategies.

Building Green: *www.buildinggreen.com* Presents the benefits of building green and resources for green products. Publishes monthly newsletter, Environmental Building News.

Center for Maximum Potential Building Systems: *www.cmpbs.org* Discusses use of life-cycle design to foster ecological balance and engages in interdisciplinary collaborations with a common vision of healthful environments, economic prosperity, and social equity. Primarily for architects and builders.

Earth Pledge: *www.earthpledge.org* Identifies and promotes innovative techniques and technologies to restore the balance between human and natural systems. Publishes books on sustainable architecture and sponsors events.

Energy Star: *www.energystar.gov* Features product lists and building resources. Site of the government-backed program that helps businesses and individuals protect the environment through superior energy efficiency.

Enterprise Foundation's Green Communities Initiative: *www.enterprisefoundation.org/ resources/green/index.asp* Highlights the Green Communities initiative to build environmentally healthy homes for low-income families and transform the way America thinks about, designs, and builds affordable communities.

Environmental Home Center: *www.environmentalhomecenter.com* Offers green building materials, including nontoxic paint, natural carpets, sustainable wood products, energy-efficient insulation, and people-friendly cleaning supplies.

GreenBlue: *www.greenblue.org*
Encourages and enables the adoption
and implementation of sustainable thinking
and design. Provides the tools required to
transform industry into an economically
profitable, ecologically regenerative, and
socially empowering activity through
intelligent design.

GreenClips: *www.greenclips.com*
Summarizes news on sustainable building
design and related government and business
issues every two weeks.

Greenguard Environmental Institute:
www.greenguard.org
Discusses healthy indoor environments,
including GEI's Greenguard Certification
Program. Provides guide to third-party-
certified low-emitting interior products and
building materials.

Healthy Building Network:
www.healthybuilding.net
Lists green building professionals,
environmental and health activists, socially
responsible investment advocates, and others
interested in promoting healthier building
materials as a means of improving public
health and preserving the global environment.

Oikos: *www.oikos.com*
Includes articles, products, and books on
green building. Publishes email news feed,
Green Building News.

Rocky Mountain Institute: *www.rmi.org*
Fosters the efficient and restorative use of
resources to make the world secure, just,
prosperous, and life-sustaining; works with
businesses, communities, individuals,
and governments to create employment,
protect natural and human capital, and
increase profit and competitive advantage,
largely by doing what they do more efficiently.

TreeHugger: *www.treehugger.com*
Promotes a modern yet environmentally
responsible aesthetic. Features news, reviews,
and recommendations for products and
services that are modern and green.

U.S. Green Building Council: *www.usgbc.org*
Brings together leaders from across the
building industry working to promote
buildings that are environmentally
responsible, profitable, and healthy places
to live and work; includes a directory of green
products and services.

Acknowledgments

This book depended upon the contributions of numerous people, to whom I'd like to give special thanks. These include the architects and other professionals I interviewed and whose stories I collected; Andrea Monfried and Stacee Lawrence, my editors at The Monacelli Press, for their strong energy; Paul Carlos, Urshula Barbour, and Mimi Jung, the graphic designers, for creating each page with care; Lisa Germany, who always knew what I wanted to say, and Susan Lauzau, who ensured correct words and structure; Cary Sullivan, for her enthusiasm for the proposal; and friends Christine Coulson and Andrea Mason, for their extraordinary insights. Endless thanks above all to my parents, for always encouraging me to put my thoughts out into the world.

Illustration Credits

Numbers refer to page numbers.

© Peter Aaron/ESTO: 16 top, 72, 90–91, 92, 93, 94, 95, 96, 97, 136, 164 bottom, 208–9, 210, 211, 213, 214, 215
Assassi: 116
Richard Barnes: 24, 158
Courtesy Barry Rice Architects: 21
Philip Beaurline: 201
Lydia Gould Bessler: 13, 144
Eric Boman: 6, 73, 174–75, 176, 177, 178, 179, 180, 181
Antoine Bootz: 126–27, 128, 129, 130, 131
Andrew Bordwin: 19 top
Ed Burtynsky: 10
Richard Cadan: 48
Courtesy Charles Rose Architects: 38, 66
Chuck Choi: 46, 49, 60–61, 62, 63, 64–65, 67
Jonn Coolidge: 109, 143, 146
James Dow: 193
Pieter Estersohn: 190
Courtesy Fairfax & Sammons: 19 bottom
Scott Frances: 8, 16 bottom, 89, 114, 132, 138, 168
© Scott Frances/ESTO: 12, 44, 118–19, 120, 121, 122–23, 124, 125, 142
Courtesy Gluckman Mayner Architects: 51
Art Grice: 23
Rheto Halm: 162, 164 top, 196 top

© Hester + Hardaway: 26–27, 28, 29, 30, 31, 33, 81, 135, 161
Douglas Hill: 150–51, 153, 154, 155, 156, 157
Tim Hursley: 50, 117, 196 bottom
Courtesy Ike Kligerman Barkley Architects: 212
Raimund Koch: 87, 98, 104
Courtesy Lake/Flato Architects: 32, 206, 207
© John Linden 2007: 37, 102, 172
Courtesy Lorcan O'Herlihy Architects: 152
Courtesy M. Finney Design and FARO Studio: 20
Michael Mundy/Courtesy Gluckman Mayner Architects: 74
Steven Vaughan Photography: 216
Tim Street-Porter: 56
Catherine Tighe: 34, 78, 88, 107, 203
Bill Timmerman: 101, 199
Courtesy Toshiko Mori Architect: 42 top
Courtesy Turner Brooks Architect: 42 bottom, 149, 182–83, 184, 185, 186–87, 188, 189
Bruce van Inwegen: 83
Jonathan Wallen: 68, 71, 84, 167, 170, 173
Paul Warchol: 40, 141, 195
Michael Weschler: 113